Virginia and Bill Cantore own and operate a frame shop in Jacksonville, Florida, where they specialize in conservation framing for collectors of fine art.

A SPECTRUM BOOK   Prentice-Hall, Inc., Englewood Cliffs, N.J. 07632

Virginia and Bill Cantore

CREATIVE PICTURE FRAMING

How to frame your artwork, needlework, mirrors, and 3-D displays

Library of Congress Cataloging in Publication Data

Cantore, Virginia.
    Creative picture framing.

    (A Spectrum Book)
    Bibliography: p.
    Includes index.
    1. Picture frames and framing.   I. Cantore,
Bill.   III. Title.
N8550.C34   749'.7   81-5886
ISBN   0-13-190645-3   AACR2
ISBN   0-13-190637-2 (pbk)

To Christopher, Anna, and Lisa, our children
and to Louise Ault

Editorial/production supervision by Louise M. Marcewicz
Interior Design by Christine Gehring Wolf
Cover Design by Ira Shapiro
Manufacturing buyer: Cathie Lenard

© 1981 by Prentice-Hall, Inc., Englewood Cliffs, New Jersey 07632

A SPECTRUM BOOK

10   9   8   7   6   5   4   3   2   1

Printed in the United States of America

PRENTICE-HALL INTERNATIONAL, INC., London
PRENTICE-HALL OF AUSTRALIA PTY. LIMITED, Sydney
PRENTICE-HALL OF CANADA, LTD., Toronto
PRENTICE-HALL OF INDIA PRIVATE LIMITED, New Delhi
PRENTICE-HALL OF JAPAN, INC., Tokyo
PRENTICE-HALL OF SOUTHEAST ASIA PTE. LTD., Singapore
WHITEHALL BOOKS LIMITED, Wellington, New Zealand

CONTENTS

PREFACE

There is a conservation movement in framing sweeping the country today through certain groups who make information available to framers through periodicals and pamphlets, and many fine framers and art galleries are educating their customers in the handling and care of their valuable collections. To "conserve," in this sense, is to maximize the life of the piece by using the proper technique of construction and the appropriate materials in framing. We hope that our book will advance this movement, helping to spread the word about correct treatment in the framing of your treasures. The object you are framing may have little value or great value, but if it is worth displaying at all, it should be framed properly to preserve it in its original condition for as many years as possible—as you know, long life is the test of any good craft. It is a surprising fact that until very recently, protective measures for preserving pictures were known to few framers, professional or otherwise, and as a result many fine or loved works have been lost to us, a result that a knowledgeable framer could so easily have prevented. Our book will emphasize proper framing of each object, with conservation measures appropriate to its value and eye training to present the object in an aesthetically pleasing manner.

To teach you most clearly the basic principles of proper framing, we have separated the kinds of things framed into four categories—works on paper, works on cloth, three-dimensional or physical objects, and rigid pieces such as mirrors. We will then present a step-by-step procedure for you to follow with each classification and give you the reasons for doing it that way. This serves to clarify the particular principle involved and to teach you the traditional method of handling the work for its most appropriate display and protection. There are variations in the preparation for framing of some of the items within a group, and we shall discuss these distinctions as well. Even if you don't do your own framing and take your work to a professional, you will be better informed about methods and materials and therefore better equipped to choose a good framer and know what you are paying for.

The art of framing pictures is a much neglected one. The difference between a well-framed picture and an ordinarily framed one is astonishing! Although there are almost unlimited approaches to the framing of any one picture, "right" framing can transform the ordinary into an object of art or set off the true artwork in full glory. This text will help to guide your choices toward enhancing the picture and prolonging its life with the proper framing. Our emphasis is on the aesthetic side of framing—that is, placement of the picture in a setting that complements it so that its full beauty may be realized—rather than on the purely technical aspects of putting the frame elements together. But technical construction is important, too, for protection and beauty. You should develop a very critical and conscientious eye in every detail, and we shall help you to do so, with tips from our own experience. There is no substitute for a clean, well-cut mat, properly centered in the frame. A frame with perfectly joined corners is a demonstration of fine craftsmanship.

In picture framing you must not be afraid to use your own ingenuity. This and any other similar instruction manual serve only as a guide to basics. If you have a better idea, try it. Even the most experienced professional picture framer has to use his or her ingenuity to solve new problems or to improve on old solutions if that person is to remain vital in the field. Use your imagination. This is a part of the art and expression of this kind of work. Framing your own picture can be fun, a delight to the eye and a feeling of accomplishment for a job well done—and done yourself! From so many possibilities you can create your own setting and truly make your treasures objects of art.

ACKNOWLEDGMENTS

Our special thanks go to Dorothy Werner, representative, Prentice-Hall, who made this project possible, and to Lynne Lumsden, our editor, for helping bring it into reality.

To Margaret Koscielny, Jeff Dunn, Jerry Dodge, and Miriam Ahrens, who helped us to gain access to many of the fine artworks reproduced in the book, we wish to express deep appreciation.

To all the collectors who graciously allowed us to reproduce their pictures, and to all who lent their work for the processes demonstrated—Janet Hall, Carolyn Smith, Irene Laffe, Michiko Frost, Vivian Fasking, Bobbi Davis, and Vivian Barr— thank you.

We are deeply grateful to Ruth Johnson, Virginia's mother, who typed the manuscript, and to her husband, George Johnson, for all his knowledge of woodworking, and for their joint sweet encouragement and enthusiasm.

It is with great pleasure that we can now express thanks to the Metropolitan Museum of Art for the museum experience that so enriched our lives and directed us into this field.

All photographs and illustrations are done by the authors.

INTRODUCTION:
WHY FRAME?

When we have acquired or made a piece of artwork of which we are especially proud, we want to display it. To do this, we put it into a frame.

The frame offers a convenient way both to view and to protect the work at the same time. Obviously the glass protects a print from humidity and atmospheric impurities, and the wooden molding provides a means for holding its contents together and for hanging. But just as a jewel is enhanced by being placed into a harmonious setting, a work of art is shown to its best advantage by being set into the appropriate frame.

FIGURE i-1.
Homemade frame. Janet Hall: Cross stitch sampler (1978).
Frame by Grandfather Wallenbruch.

Not every artwork needs to be framed in order to protect it. A painting, because of its composition of permanent elements and its final varnish, which serves the same protective purpose as glass, uses a frame largely for enhancement. On the other hand, drawings, watercolors, and various papers are fragile and use frames not only for enhancement but for special protection while being viewed. In both cases the frame acts as a setting for the work as it is being exhibited.

Early in the history of Western culture, paintings in a form called fresco were done directly on the walls of the surroundings in which they were meant to be seen—cathedrals and palaces, for

Introduction: Why
Frame?

example—imbuing the surroundings with a spirit of beauty and meaning for those who entered. Here the completed work was made by the artist, designed for this space and with this particular environment in mind. Usually the artist designed the painting for a special area, which was framed by the architectural elements, or sometimes a permanent decorative design in the form of a mosaic or other material was installed around the picture as an offsetting border, making the whole piece a permanent part of the wall.

It was not until around the thirteenth century, when the artist began to do the completed painting in the studio for later transport and placement into another location, that the frame as we know it came into being. The earliest portable frame was really a physical part of the painting. The painting was done in the hollowed-out center of a flat panel, the outer raised edges forming the frame. Later, when it was discovered that a separate frame helped to prevent warpage of the panel, this frame was constructed and decorated by the individual painter or by craftspeople. They designed and built this "setting" around the painting to suit the area it was to occupy, usually in a form echoing the architecture of the building, such as a small replica of the portal (doorway) of the building. In fact this early form of the frame existed for several centuries, having the distinct significance the frame carries even today, of being a doorway from the outer world of reality into the inner world of the painting. Once executed, the whole portable piece was then carried and placed into the particular environment for which it was commissioned. With the discovery of molding in the fifteenth century, styles in framing changed to resemble more closely our modern-day conception of the frame. Until this time the frame had been considered to be an intrinsic part of the painting and held a not less important stature, the two parts being considered one object.

For centuries all the preliminary sketches of artists were considered studies and were discarded. The earliest preserved examples of artists' studies on paper date from the mid-fourteenth century, when the need arose for art students to copy the sketches of their masters. Before this time only the finished painting was felt to be of importance, but with the new interest in the details of nature, and especially the human figure, that stirred in the early Renaissance, the spontaneity and freshness of drawings as well as their informative detail gave rise to an increasing number of collectors.

By the sixteenth century, art lovers as well as students and scholars were collecting the drawings of the masters they admired. These works were preserved in folios, just as the early illuminated manuscripts and other illustrated written materials were preserved in books. These were never exhibited but were opened and viewed privately.

The framing of these works on paper did not develop until relatively recent times. Factors such as the ever increasing importance attached to these drawings and sketches, the development of the printing process (wood engravings which could reproduce paintings and etchings, for example) and the new medium of watercolor combined to make artwork on paper appreciated for its own sake, as an end in itself. In the middle of the eighteenth century in France the first public exhibitions of framed drawings were held. It was around this time that the desire for more frequent viewing of the collected works, not to mention their merchandising, gave rise to the widespread framing and exhibition of drawings, woodcuts, etchings, colored engravings, and watercolors, especially in France and England. The frames for these works were smaller versions of those used for oils, and as time went on, they were further simplified to small woods, often dark without gold leaf and with understated, little, or no carving. This simplicity was due partly to the feeling that these works were less important than paintings, partly to the more intimate surroundings in which they were displayed (in studies, libraries, and halls), and largely to the more delicate nature of the work. In more contemporary times works on paper have assumed an importance equal to that of paintings, and drawings by masters are shown in important places side by side with paintings and in equally elaborate frames. Glass was always the protective agent.

Another decisive factor in the widespread framing of paperworks was expense. Drawings and prints were less expensive than paintings, and therefore more accessible for decorating the rooms of less wealthy households. So the common people, who could not afford the services of craftsmen to construct their frames, built their own. By the late eighteenth century the decorating of walls with artwork and homespun crafts was common, even in humble homes. The colonists in America adorned their walls with needlework, naive paintings, maps, and verse. The frames were like the pieces they encased, only more or less crude, depending on the skill or wealth of the homeowner.

In modern times, with fashion moving toward the functional and the geometric, we have eliminated much of the decorative quality from our environment and have adopted a simplicity of means. Our buildings and furnishings are more streamlined, designed with their function in mind and on the premise that "if it works, it is beautiful." So it is with the framing of contemporary art. A simple edging of wood or metal has come into vogue. The frame serves its function by providing a simple delineation of its subject. Throughout history styles have changed in conformity with the prevailing tastes of the times. When a society has been intellectual, the decorative forms used were that of a more geometric nature, and when a society relied on the emotions, the patterns were more floral or arabesque.

The function of the frame is to display the work while protecting it. Although the frame is not really an intrinsic part of a work of art and the choices of its makeup are unlimited, once added it becomes an extension of the artwork, and this union must be so integrated, so totally right, that the eye will not be aware that it is two separate parts. The frame must be as compatible and consistent with the piece as possible and offer an offsetting, harmonious beauty to it as well as to the decor in which it is placed. Although the frame is ever changing, it still functions as a portal of its time, facilitating the transition from the real world of the environment into the imaginary world of the object of art.

1
WORKS ON PAPER

Any work on paper, whether it is a drawing, a print, a watercolor, a document, a map, a photograph, or whatever, is framed under glass or an acrylic sheet (Plexiglas) and usually with a mat or shadow-boxing technique for removing the glass from the surface of the picture. It is supported inside the frame by a backing, usually a paper one called a mounting board. There is very little written for the layman that treats the framing of paperwork separately, and it is because this is the subject most often framed and most easily damaged by improper framing that we emphasize it in these pages.

FIGURE 1-1.
Henri de Toulouse-Lautrec: "Jeanne Hading." Lithograph (one of twenty on white board) (1895). Private collection, Jacksonville, Florida.

CONSIDERING VALUE

When you are about to frame a piece of work on a paper base, it is important for you to realize exactly what it is and what value it has, not only to you but in the present and future market. This is so because in the framing of papers one has options. Although the basic method of framing is the same for all papers—glass, mat, and frame—the materials and treatment should be chosen in full knowledge of the work's value and of the appropriate materials and treatment. We must learn to distinguish between works that should be preserved and those that need not be, and use the right approach in either case.

Some papers should be permanently mounted, that is, pasted entirely to a stiff backing, in order to have the best appearance in frames. For others this form of mounting could be disastrous, not only because of the tendency of the work to discolor through the years when mounted, but because of the loss of market value. It is enough to hinge and mat some works with a sheet of good drawing paper as a backing, but for others completely acid-free matting and backing are called for.

Until very recent times works on paper, other than those of the most important artists, were not deemed to be of great value. For example, drawings of the lesser masters of great periods were sold for practically nothing even as late as the 1950s. So little value was attached to those works that many of them have been damaged or lost to us altogether through improper handling and framing methods. Today we have easy access to conservation materials such as museum board for matting and backing, and when these precautionary measures seem to be called for, they should be used in framing.

Of course the terms "value" and "expense" are relative, and in most cases you will use your own common sense concerning the pieces that should be handled with their longer-term preservation in mind. The following three divisions offer guidelines for identifying and handling the various kinds of work on paper.

INEXPENSIVE PRINTS AND POSTERS

In general the prints we would call inexpensive are the kinds that are mass-produced commercially and are widely available. They are reproductions of original works, which can range from the glossy, thin papers of the type found in magazines or calendars to those reproduced more carefully on better paper and with closer resemblance to the original artwork. Usually the publisher's name and some identifying data about the artist and the original work are printed at the bottom, but these prints are not signed individually by the artist. This group does not include antique reproductions, which we would consider to be in the class of more valuable work.

Since these prints or posters are usually framed as color notes for decorative purposes or as reflections of one's taste in the home or office and are not to be preserved for future handing down or sale, they should be permanently wet- or dry-mounted in order to present a neat, smooth appearance inside the frame. To mount a paper permanently is to paste it to a stiff backing, a mounting board, so that it will lie perfectly flat inside the frame without ripples or bulges. Without being mounted in this way, many papers show a ripple sooner or later, especially the lighter-bodied ones. This is very disturbing to some people and not necessary when you are framing an inexpensive print.

Photographs, except for fine art photos, are also handled in this way.

PAPERS OF SENTIMENTAL VALUE

Many of the paperworks you would like to frame are neither mass-produced prints nor investment-quality artwork and seem to fall somewhere in between. You may have a watercolor or drawing of your own or of a friend or family member. Perhaps there is a letter, card, or commendation of some sort, something of sentimental value, even your diploma. Sometimes if you take a little extra care in the framing of these "middle value" pieces, you will be glad you did, for the years pass quickly, and acid stains or other stains from impurities in the backing or adhering tape show their marks in a very short time. Probably any work on good paper should be framed with good materials. Here is an important set of rules to follow in the framing of anything on paper:

- NEVER USE CORRUGATED BOARD, MASKING TAPE, OR SCOTCH TAPE DIRECTLY IN CONTACT WITH THE PIECE FRAMED. These materials have remarkable staining power and are the worst enemies of paper in framing (and are, incidentally, the materials most commonly used).

- DO NOT GLUE DOWN ALL THE EDGES OF THE PAPER IN AN ATTEMPT TO FLATTEN IT. This will cause uneven tensions in the paper, resulting in a bubble at the center. Hinge the piece from the top and let it drape, unless you are mounting it permanently to the backing.

- SET THE PIECE AWAY FROM THE GLASS BY USING A MAT OR SHADOW BOX TECHNIQUE. (See Chapter 3.) Changes in temperature can cause a condensation of water inside the glass, which could result in moisture damage to the paper or make for favorable conditions for mildew or other fungus growth.

- SEAL THE BACK OF YOUR COMPLETED FRAME JOB AS WELL AS POSSIBLE TO KEEP OUT AIR AND MOISTURE. This sealing is not the same as the final paper "dust cover," but is accomplished by taping the outer stiff backing all around the edges to the back of the frame. (See Fig. 1-21.)

The manufacturers of wood-pulp papers use one of two processes for breaking down the wood chips or other material the paper is made from—either an acid process or an alkaline process. Before the pulp is molded into sheets, it is subjected to washings to bring the pH factor (balance between acid and alkali) to as near neutral as possible. These papers are the ones that make up the bulk of all the paper products we use, including cardboard and corrugated board, the white papers having been bleached and the brown and gray ones left in their natural color. Single-ply papers—those used in corrugated boards, and poster boards, and bond papers—do not usually contain excesses of acid or alkaline residue in themselves, but the adhesive and sizing (stiffener) used in manufacturing these products can often be high in acidity. The silicate adhesive used to make corrugated board is an acid substance that is particularly vulnerable to moisture or humidity and that can bleed through the paper, causing a stain and a brittleness to the artwork. Gray cardboard is made from wood pulp too, but also from pulverized recycled waste, and can contain impurities such as rubber bands and paper clips, particles that can stain or damage artwork.

The backing that supports your work is the most important, since the whole picture touches it. Always use a white backing; the better the backing, the more years it will protect your work. You may use a piece of bond paper, a mat board, an illustration board, a rag (all-cotton) charcoal or drawing paper, or a watercolor paper. Better still, use a piece of the same paper the work itself is done on. Then hinge the work onto the backing with pieces of rice paper and library paste. (We discuss the method of doing this in our section on matting.)

We have seen so many nice drawings and documents that have

been framed with corrugated board or cardboard backings and have turned brown and brittle as if burned. One very obvious example was a diploma that wasn't even framed, but had been rolled up in a cardboard tube for thirteen years. When we unrolled it, the entire section that had been touching the tube was brown, and the part that was resting on the inside was white. It was half brown and half white!

For still better preservation you may purchase, in artists' supply stores, barrier paper, two-ply museum board, or other backings with a neutral pH factor designed for the purpose of moderate conservation. In framing, it is best to have one backing next to the work, to which it is usually attached, then one or two stiff backings to insulate and support the work still further. (See Fig. 1-12.) A very fine and versatile board for the final stiff backing of any quality work is Fome-Cor board. It is a rigid, lightweight board, usually 1/4 inch (6.35 mm) thick, that is made of a polystyrene layer sandwiched between two smooth craft papers. Unlike corrugated board, the layers are pressed together with heat and no acid-containing adhesive. This is not to indicate that it should replace an acid-free backing next to your work, but it should serve the purpose of final stiff backing. With proper sealing, Fome-Cor will help keep moisture from your work inside the finished frame in much the way medicines are kept fresh with the use of a small piece of cotton or styrofoam inside the bottle. Fome-Cor has a thousand uses in framing and is really worth trying. It is sold in art supply stores.

Masking tape and Scotch tape not only impart stains and rips in their removal but also tend to dry out and let the picture slip out of place. Rice paper hinges with library paste are economical and have no such tendencies. "Rice" paper, or Japanese mulberry paper, can be purchased in art supply stores, and library paste in office supply stores.

We have stressed that wet or dry mounting will decrease the life expectancy of papers mainly to warn you that valuable papers should not be mounted. However, if you find that a work that you are framing, such as a watercolor, is much too rippled for your taste, and if the work is in the questionable range of monetary value, you can mount it in a relatively acid-free manner onto a mounting board with a rag surface (or an artists' illustration board, available in art supply stores), using wheat paste (a method we discuss in the section on wet mounting).

Just one step below real museum framing, which we discuss next, is to use two-ply museum board or its equivalent directly in back of your work, along with the acid-free hinges described, an inner lining of barrier paper or two-ply museum board on the part of the mat that will touch the picture, and a Fome-Cor stiff backing.

A final word—about diplomas. Your diploma is that oft-neglected certificate of accomplishment that may seem of little importance in early life when you are at the starting line of dynamic achievement but may be prized in years to come. Either of two simple precautionary measures in keeping or framing can preserve this fine personal commendation for a lifetime: (a) flat-storing it in a drawer between two good pieces of paper; or (b) hinging it to a conservation backing inside a frame. Unless you make a special request for other treatment, most professional picture framers will dry-mount your diploma as standard procedure, and while this is no real disaster, the certificate will retain its original appearance for many, many years if you will follow our instructions for the framing of papers with moderate conservation.

INVESTMENT-QUALITY WORK ON PAPER

Framers and the public at large are far more aware now than ever before of conservation. To preserve our own artwork or collected artwork is of great interest to us all.

Just as you must use glass over papers in framing to protect them from moisture and impurities in the air, you must use neutral-pH-factor mats, backings, and adhesives in the framing of very fine papers to prevent their contact with acid or other damaging chemicals. There are now on the market fine framing materials for this purpose—two- and four-ply museum boards that are 100 percent rag (made of cotton fibers), as well as other conservation mats and backings made by reputable manufacturers, and all are accessible to you, the consumer.

The monetary value of an artwork or other matter on paper depends entirely upon the highest amount of money someone is willing to pay for it; in other words, the "highest bid" is the value. You may put any price on an artwork, but what it will fetch in the general market is the true worth at the time, and worth does change. Very valuable papers are those that are rare and important, either historically or artistically. Antique maps, documents, and artworks, even old prints, such as those by Currier and Ives, that have become collectors' items because of their age or historic significance are in this category, as are the original works of internationally recognized artists, past or present. Any other paper you may have, such as a limited-edition print or a watercolor by an artist of little renown, is purely speculative in the investment field, but you may choose to frame it with protective measures and later be glad you did. It is an inexpensive enough little "insurance policy" to use a museum board. If you don't know the work's present market value, you will have to rely upon the dealer who sold it to you, or, for the best analysis, you may consult an expert in the field.

Just as in all the arts—writing, music, film, sculpture, painting—some works on paper are simply not worth the expense of preserving for future generations, and you should develop judgment in this. Museum or conservation framing is necessary only for the long-term preservation of artwork or other valuable papers and probably should be done by a reputable professional framer who specializes in this field. Here we will describe the materials used if you do wish to do it yourself or know how it is done and the kinds of paperwork we would consider to merit this fine treatment.

One problem we often encounter in museum framing is the reluctance on the part of the customer to accept the ripples that are almost inevitable, at least to some extent, in a piece of paper that has not been permanently wet- or dry-mounted. If you are to collect and frame fine artwork, you must reconcile yourself to this inevitability and realize that rippling is natural to paper, and is not necessarily the result of improper treatment by the framer. If you will attend fine exhibitions, you will see that ripply paperwork is common in museums and fine collections everywhere. A case in point was brought to our attention recently by a collector who, years ago in Japan, had procured three original Hokusai woodcuts, which he had brought home and had had framed by a professional. After some time he was interested in having his prints appraised, and in the inquiry it was discovered that they had been dry-mounted in the framing process. The appraiser told him that since there were many other prints like his that had not been mounted, his were of far less value than they would otherwise have been.

In our own framing operation a customer once brought us two Currier and Ives prints to be reframed. When we took them out of the original frames, we found that one had been placed directly against a wood backing, and the other, a corrugated board. Both had yellowed considerably, but the one with the corrugated board, probably much more recently framed, was far more brittle and stained than the other one. In still another instance, where the artist had done his own framing a few years previously, a fine acrylic painting on rag paper was brought in because it had slipped out of place in the mat. When we took it out, we found that it was backed with corrugated board, which had already begun to cause stains on the back surface of the paper.

ORIGINAL ARTWORK. Drawings, watercolors, pastel paintings, and now acrylic paintings on paper by famous artists are prized by collectors, and if by chance you are fortunate enough to own one, you must take full precautionary measures in framing.

ANTIQUE PAPERS OR MODERN DOCUMENTS AND LETTERS. Old maps can be very valuable, and some collectors specialize in them. Many of them have been preserved in books for centuries and are in astonishingly good condition. It is well to note that any paper is really best conserved in a flat portfolio, away from light, heat, or humidity, with only acid-free sheets touching it.

Other antique documents or prints are also valuable because of their age or historic significance, such as the early wood engravings that served as reproductions of paintings or as book illustrations. With our interest in the past, early family documents such as land grants or family trees fall into the Very Valuable category.

If you happen to possess a letter or document signed by an important person on the national and international scene and you wish to frame it for your home or office, you should use the same conservation methods you would use for any fine artwork on paper. Unlike some other papers, documents have always been done on fine paper and have their own natural preservation built in. If framed properly and given proper care, they can be preserved indefinitely.

ORIGINAL PRINTS. Most of us are not likely to own a great-master drawing or watercolor, as even museums are finding it difficult to afford them. But we still have access to original prints by fine artists, both old ones and new ones. An original print, unlike the mass-produced commercial kind of print, is not one that is reproduced from an original artwork of another medium, such as an oil painting or a pastel, but is designed and planned by the artist for the printing medium, such as an etching, serigraph (silk screen), woodcut, or lithograph. Again the valuable ones are designed by internationally known artists and are produced in relatively few numbers, thus the name LIMITED EDITION. The artist personally oversees the printing of the edition and will stop the printing once the plate lacks the clarity of line or richness of color he or she finds accept-able. After this number, usually not more than one hundred or so prints, depending on the process, the plate is destroyed or can-celed. The artist will usually number the prints in pencil at the bottom and sign some or all of them. In the market, the signed and numbered ones are of most value.

Contemporary original prints are usually done on fine, rather heavy-bodied cotton paper made by Arches, Rives, or other fine specialty papermakers. You can usually recognize a fine paper by its watermark, that is, letters or emblems that appear in the paper itself when it is held up to the light, and by its deckle edges. Etchings and woodcuts are easily recognized by clear inden-tation in the paper made by the plate or woodblock in printing, because they are done on rather soft, absorbent paper, into which the image is imprinted by pressure. Silk screens have velvety, matte, opaque colors. Original lithographs are a little more difficult to identify by the untrained eye and can resemble drawings or transparent and opaque watercolors. Because of its versatility, the lithograph process is widely used by commercial printers too, but this kind of lithograph is a photoreproduction process. Colored lithographs have uneven light dispersion on the surface of the paper and often an oily residue on the back coming through the paper.

Older original prints were done on handmade paper without the watermarks we know today, and many very fine woodcuts were and are still done on rice paper, especially by the Japanese. Many of the original prints that predate the twentieth century were neither signed nor numbered.

All very valuable papers should be framed with four-ply museum-board (or its equivalent) mats and backing, acid-free hinges, glass, frame, and preferably fine, stiff outer backing materials such as Fome-Cor, and they should be well sealed. You must never mount them permanently to the backing, trim them, or alter them in any way. They should be kept in relatively dark areas to avoid light damage, in low humidity, away from heat or any extremes in temperature. It is only for the viewing that papers are framed. Really the best conservation is to keep them in portfolios with only acid-free materials touching them, which is what museum framing most closely approximates. The ultraviolet rays in sunlight and fluorescent light are very destructive to papers, and there are now forms of Plexiglas that have ultraviolet filters, available at very high prices. In predicting the future, we are certain that filters of ultraviolet rays will be developed and perfected in glass and Plexiglas to be employed in conservation framing and, with the new acid-free materials we see invented every day, that better boards and adhesives will be more and more in use for framing.

SELECTING THE PROPER MAT AND FRAME

Although there have been periods in certain areas of the world when one basic frame type was considered to be the right one, and there probably are still countries in which this idea prevails, nowadays in the West we have an almost unlimited selection. It is our task in this book to offer some basic axioms to help direct you toward more aesthetically pleasing choices. But let us note too that changing times and the development of new materials dictate certain fashions in this as well as in other fields, so that what is the rule today may be far from acceptable tomorrow. In all our talk of aesthetics and the guidelines we present, you must let your eyes be the final judge of rightness or wrongness. An ancient Zen proverb cautions, "Do not mistake the pointing finger for the moon." Rules in the aesthetics of this or any other of the arts are pointing fingers. Learn to trust your own eyes.

The mat in picture framing is that colored cardboard out of which a window is cut to surround the picture, allowing for an offsetting expanse between picture and frame and a separation between picture and glass. The mat serves a dual purpose—that of enhancing and that of protecting. It is designed to use on paperworks, not paintings, needlework, or any other material. Mat boards can be bought in art supply stores and are available in a rainbow of colors, many textures, and also in fabric-covered form. The standard size of mat board is 32 inches by 40 inches (81.3 cm × 101.6 cm). Although you may purchase precut mats in all the standard picture-frame sizes, you will save money and have a much wider variety of size and shape, as well as better-quality board, by learning to cut your own.

Choosing the proper mat color for your picture can be very challenging, but with repeated practice, anyone can learn to choose nice harmonies and offsetting contrasts, training the eye to see what is really there and checking the sight with one's inner reaction. We all have an inner sense of visual rightness, of which we must become aware and which we must cultivate. This is the aesthetic sense. This can be easily illustrated by considering things we see every day, such as the way people dress. When we see a person dressed in a totally inharmonious manner, say in a bright green and orange boldly patterned shirt and softly flowered pink pastel pants, our inner aesthetic sense is offended. If, on the other hand, we see someone in a harmoniously colored suit or correctly contrasting shirt and pants, we have an inner sense of pleasure in the sight and an assent, or silently felt yes, in its rightness. Learn to listen to this inner assent or yes in picture framing.

Choosing the right frame is again an intuitive process in terms of what "works" with the picture, mat color, and room surroundings. If you are framing a picture of another period, it can be fun and interesting to study the history of frames to see how the picture would have been presented in its day. However, this is not necessary, since a mixture of periods is widely accepted today.

MAT COLOR AND TEXTURE

One needn't know very much color theory in the choosing of a colored mat, because the seeing and the sense of rightness are all that really matter. As in every other field, the more experience you have in choosing mats, the more readily you can identify what pleases you and what you can best live with. We all react differently to colors, and our seeing carries mental connotations, or prejudices. The color red, for example, may conjure up a very pleasant, warm feeling in one person and the complete opposite in another. Black or gray may be an exciting visual choice for a picture, but may carry an undesirable feeling for some people. Luckily every picture has more than one possibility in using a mat; there is no one right way. This leeway helps you to coordinate the picture with your room and follow your personal preference, which is yet another of the mat's attributes (in addition to protecting and enhancing the picture).

A basic knowledge of some good color harmonies may prove helpful in choosing mats, and when you are trying out mat colors, let your eyes test this knowledge. The primary colors, those from which all other colors can be made, are red, yellow, and blue. From these we can mix the secondary colors—orange, green, and violet. This group plus further mixtures make up the color wheel (Fig. 1-2). Moving around the color wheel, taking any one-

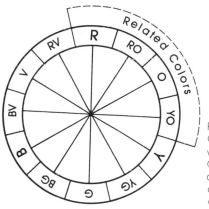

FIGURE 1-2.
Color wheel. Any one-third of the color wheel in a segment contains related colors. Opposite colors on the color wheel are complementaries. Both of these made good color harmonies and can be useful in choosing mats.

third of the wheel in a segment, we have what are called related colors, that is, all of these colors contain one color in common. For instance, red, red-orange, orange, and yellow-orange all contain red. Related colors always make good harmonies. Directly across from any color on the color wheel is its complement, such as red-green, yellow-violet, and blue-orange. These colors in the proper proportions, that is, the dominating color plus a smaller amount of its complement for accent, also make good harmony. This is useful to know in choosing the inner part of a double mat. A third and more elementary way to achieve perfect color harmony is the use of shades or tints of one color, that is, the color mixed with black or white, respectively. Of course the easiest and most often practiced way to choose a harmonious mat is to "pick up" one of the colors in the picture itself. The other three ways we have mentioned to achieve harmony—related colors, complementary colors, and shades or tints—are useful tools in choosing a mat with color contrast.

Besides color harmony, a very important consideration in matting is color value. Value in color is the relative lightness or darkness of the color, and you might think of it as if you were looking at a black and white photograph of the color with no knowledge of its hue. In the spectrum, pale yellow has a lighter value than deep blue, but grayed yellow ochre has a deeper value than pastel blue. In choosing mats, the proper color value is actually more important than the color itself. You can see this by choosing a completely incorrect color with the right value and comparing it with a mat of the right color but wrong value. Too light or too dark a value in mat color will wash out or deaden the picture, or will merely sit there with no relationship to it. The correct value will enliven the piece, even if it is not the right color. In matting artwork, it is usually a good rule not to use a color darker than the darkest dark nor lighter than the lightest light in the picture. There are exceptions to this rule, however; one being those grayed middle-value pictures that are altogether brought to life by a very light mat or dramatized by a very dark mat, but made dreadfully dull by anything in between.

Always think of where you are planning to hang your framed work in terms of the color scheme and general decor when you choose your mat and frame. Any mat color should be harmonious with its surroundings as well as with the picture. If the color that goes best with your room is in conflict with the picture to be matted, then you probably have the wrong picture for that room. Perhaps you can approach the matting from a neutral point of view in this case, with a small inner mat of some room color.

Blues, greens, and their related colors are cool and tend to recede in space visually. Reds, oranges, and yellows are warm and seem to come forward. Take your cue from the artwork itself when you pick out the mat. If the overall tones in the work are cool, it is usually better to stay with cool tones; if warm, warm tones. If the colors are vivid and intense, use a bright mat color or white. Sometimes you may pick up a small area of color in the picture by using a similar mat color, but in that case guard against too large an area of matting, which would contend with the overall dominance of one color in the picture and upset the balance achieved by the artist. For instance, if the artist's color scheme consists of an overall green with a small accent of red, a wide red mat can throw the whole color composition out of balance. Likewise a mat of the same color as the overall picture can be too much of a good thing. Remember, your mat will bring out areas in the picture, so be careful what you bring out and try to keep in tune with the artist's intention. The mat is the accompanist to set off the soloist—the picture. Let it further heighten the feeling expressed by the colors in the picture.

Be careful with the use of blue mats, employing them only in those cases in which you are positive they are right, because some blues have a tendency to be undefined by the eye and to recede and expand visually, giving the picture an appearance of floating in space. This is especially true of the blue-violets. Be careful also with colors like pink, pale yellows, and pastels, which may give the picture too sweet a look. In the use of double mats, it is usually best to have good contrast between the two colors. When double-matting a dark picture, the inner mat should be the lighter one; and conversely when double-matting a light picture, the inner mat should be the darker one.

Strong or boldly designed work or work with active or big forms will often need a dark, bright, or strongly contrasting mat color, as in a highly contrasting double mat to delineate and contain the image. Be bold with bold pictures and gentle with gentle pictures. Delicate work, such as pen and ink, will require a lighter color mat, and a very small area of inner mat if double-matted, say 1/8 inch (3.175 mm) of inner mat showing. Similarly, textures in mats also follow suit: stronger textures, such as burlap, on stronger work delicate textures, such as silk, on quieter work. Black is mysterious and rich, but in large size overpowering to very light-background, delicate work. It should be used on dark, mysterious pieces; bold black-and-white work; or quiet, nocturnal scenes such as silhouetted work. Misty or ethereal pictures usually look best with wide single mats of light, grayed tones, unlike more well-defined pictures, which seem to call for very definite borders. Earthy work, such as landscapes or wildlife, seem to require the greens or browns, which are earthy colors. Basically, good choices in framing boil down to good taste.

It is always safe and in good taste to use neutral colors in matting, from white all the way across the scale to black and sometimes beige. On fine art pieces we would always recommend the use of neutral mats, for you should not add anything to the work itself, as a colored mat always does. Conservation museum boards have been available only in neutrals until recently, and most museums and many knowledgeable collectors use neutral settings to display their treasures on paper.

To choose your mat color, you may or may not have access to samples of mat board. Some art supply stores and frame shops have corner samples for you to use when buying your mat board, and these are naturally the best and easiest way to know what is available and how it looks. (Some of these shops will sell you their small scraps, incidentally.) If you are able to select from the store's mat corners, always take your work to be framed along with you in order to see what the color actually looks like on it. If you have no such convenience, then you will have to make a scrapbook of colored papers of all kinds, large and small, which you should file according to color, tint, shade, and tone (color with gray added), in an orderly fashion, as in the color wheel. It is a great eye trainer to have a file of this kind, trying different combinations to see what colors do when put either side by side, overlapping, or small on large. It helps develop color perception too. You'd be surprised at the seemingly infinite number of subtle color differences. It is also a great patience saver for your art supply dealer for you to have at least some notion of what you want before you enter his or her shop.

THE RIGHT FRAME

The frame is the showcase for your artwork and should function not only as the practical bordering device it is but as an outer extension of the artwork itself, reflecting in some way the shapes and colors expressed by its subject, the picture. A hint we might add here is that the best results in picture framing are achieved when a certain boldness of approach is employed. Fussing too long over the selections can cause a timid, noncommittal look to the project. Again, in the choices, listen for that inner assent of rightness, which you will learn to know more and more with practice. Ideally, the frame should be chosen only to enhance the picture, but in actuality it must be compatible with the surroundings as well and bring the picture into harmony with the room. Not that it has to be the same color, finish, and style as the furnishings, just in keeping with them, following the dictates of good taste. Consider your picture the priority in choosing the frame and the room a close second. Fortunately, as in matting, there are many possible answers to the frame choice, and you can usually strike a happy balance between picture and room. In choosing the frame, you must consider its size or visual weight, its shape or style, its color, and its finish.

The size of the frame or its degree of delicacy or heaviness must be determined with relation to the picture. You should "weigh" the picture visually to find the appropriate width or heaviness. Pictures with large or boldly rendered forms are heavier visually than those with airy, delicate ones. Likewise pictures with an appearance of movement or activity seem heavier than those with a sense of calm. Frames have visual weight too, apart from obvious physical size, and often a small frame can have a quite massive appearance. A deeply carved frame looks heavier than a simple or delicately carved one of the same size. A dark finish appears heavier than a light-colored one. Choose the frame that gives the picture's visual weight adequate support (perhaps even a little more than adequate) without being overly heavy itself. Practically speaking, incidentally, for good construction you will have to choose a molding of the proper physical weight as well, to be certain it is capable of holding artwork and glass for many years. The fact that the frame should enhance and set off the work without calling attention to itself does not mean that you should underestimate its value to the picture. So often we hear the expression "I don't want the frame to take away from the picture." This is probably a reaction in part to some periods in the past when indeed the framing was so ostentatious as to obliterate completely any feelings expressed in the picture. However, it must be remembered that the frame's size or ornament must not be so understated that it is inconsistent with the piece or does not perform its function, which is to provide staging. Small pictures may need expanse in framing, with a proportionally very wide mat or frame to give them their proper importance and attention. And in fact "important" artwork needs an important frame (Fig. 1-3). Too little or understated framing is as much an injustice to the subject as too much framing.

FIGURE 1-3.
Pablo Picasso: "Portrait of Jacqueline." Three-color lithograph (1956). Collection: M. Anwar Kamal.

The long strips of shaped wood (or other material such as metal) that frames are made of are called MOLDINGS. In the framing of work on paper, where you are using a mat, you can achieve width with a wide mat and a narrow molding or, conversely, with a narrow mat and a wide molding. There should be a marked difference between the widths of mat and molding, or the repetition will be tedious and aesthetically unsatisfying. Most works on paper, such as watercolors and etchings, tend to be more delicate than oil paintings and look best with smaller frames and relatively wide mats. However, if you are framing a reproduction of an oil, for the best effect you will probably want the frame to be proportionally as heavy as one that would be used on the original painting.

The shapes of moldings are flat or round, scoop or reverse, and combinations or variations of these. Observe in Figure 1-19 the profiles of common frame moldings. The profile is a cross-section of the molding, a line drawing of which is shown in Figure 1-17, and is instantly recognized by the framer or builder as the molding's shape. Flat, or panel, frames were the first type used and are really the most elementary. Now we would use them to emphasize angularity or flatness of design in the picture itself. Remember that the very early Christian works before the Renaissance were flat designs without perspective, as were the primitive paintings in colonial North America. The flat frame is very complementary to these, as well as to needleworks and modern angular abstractions. It has the characteristic also of pointing outward at the corners, evoking a feeling of extended space, which makes it suited for landscapes or seascapes, which seem to call for expanding rather than confining boundaries.

Frames that have rounded or curved shapes are often used on delicate or less defined work, such as Oriental paintings, or on pictures with rounded or curved forms. One variation of the round shape is called the S-curve, and another the swan—graceful and gentle Oriental inventions that lend themselves to florals as well as to Far Eastern subjects. (See Fig. 1-8.)

The scoop shape is the one that leads in to the picture, that is, its outer edge is away from the wall and its inner edge leads in to the picture. This kind of frame is one that emphasizes a three-dimensional quality in the picture and lends accent to depth in space. Thus it is very suitable for the traditional pictures with perspective done since the Renaissance. It also gives a feeling of intimacy, gently encompassing a portrait or interior scene, leading the eye from the outer world into the inner world of the picture (Fig. 1-4).

Reverse frames are those that extend from the picture plane and slope backward to the wall, making the picture come forward and the frame go back. This shape is definitely one to emphasize flatness of design, such as work of the Cubists and artists of succeeding schools. These artists emphatically remind us that the painting has a flat surface and that paint and design rather than subject depicted are of the utmost importance in art. The literal shoving forward of the flat picture plane tends to reinforce this feeling. A variation of the reverse frame known as a cap or box is made to accommodate the thickness of stretcher strips for canvases or for framing objects in a shadow box, but can be used in framing paper to add substance to the work or to add body for

FIGURE 1-4.
George Ault: "Still Life—Cactus." Pencil drawing (1932).
Collection of authors.

holding a heavy glass while still presenting a narrow appearance in front.

The frame's shape should be dictated by the forms in the picture—angular on straight-line work, curved on rounded forms—and should serve a sort of echo function of the picture itself. You should also consider the frame's ornamentation. A gently carved or modestly decorated frame can add interest to an otherwise too simple, unfinished look. Deeply carved moldings should be used only on very powerfully rendered work.

The color of the frame can be of various wood tones from blonde to ebony; it can be silver or gold; it can be a painted color; or it can be made up of any two or more of these elements combined. You will have to take the mat color into account when choosing the frame for work on paper (unlike oil or acrylic paintings), and their two colors should be in keeping with the cool or warm tones of the artwork. Usually it is best to have value distinction between the mat and the frame; that is, one should be darker than the other, so that they both will be clearly defined even if they are in the same color family. If you are using a dark mat, use a lighter frame, or if a light mat, a darker frame. Frame colors, even if they are "wood" colors, have the characteristics of warmth or coolness. Warm-color frames are gold, or wood tones that have a tendency toward red, yellow, or orange, whereas cool frames are silver, black, white, or lean toward the gray. Sometimes a warm color like gold is cooled off with an antiquing gray wash, which can be the answer if you need a cool frame for the picture and a gold frame for the room.

Pictures are made up of either predominantly warm or predominantly cool colors. Sometimes this is not readily apparent, and you must study the work a bit. If the piece is made up entirely of cool colors, such as a blue ink drawing on white paper, you would use a cool mat (blue) and a cool frame (silver); whereas on an all red-orange-yellow composition you would use a warm color combination of mat and frame. In either case you really don't have much choice. However, most pictures contain an offsetting warm or cool accent, which lends more leeway. You may choose to pick up this note in the mat or frame and let the other carry the predominant color or warm theme, if this will be complementary to the picture and knit it to the environment.

The silver metal-strip frame is an exception to this warm-on-warm, and cool-on-cool concept and seems to be a complement to both. Perhaps it is appropriate on warm or cool pictures because it acts as a small mirror surface and has no "permanent" appearance, or perhaps its small size is a relief to an all warm-color work. It should only be used in compatible surroundings.

In addition to the molding's style, size, and color, there is its finish to consider. Finishes can be either shiny or matte and on either rough or smooth grounds. Preferences here are much a matter of taste and trend. The prevalent inclination today is to prefer a natural look to the frame. We want metal to look like metal, wood to look like wood—and, ironically, an old-style frame to look old! We even like "real plastic," as an artist friend of ours puts it. The only really shiny frames we find acceptable are either all metal or glossy-finished woods, which are reproductions of the period frames in which this finish truly was the fashion, for example, the shiny dark wood finishes so prized by the Dutch in the seventeenth century. Gold leaf and its substitute, metal leaf, is by nature highly glossy and bright, but we accept it only after it has been "aged" with layers of antiquing. In its natural state it is too eye-catching to be suitable for most of our artwork. Matte or semigloss finishes are more popular in wood and metal-leaf frames, leaving the high-gloss finishes to the all-metal and period styles.

The frame's texture, its smoothness or roughness, is chosen to heighten the feelings of the work. The smooth frame would be used on noncomplex, smoothly blended work or clean, hard-edge work, for instance. It presents the picture with as little interference from the frame as possible. Rough textures are often used in a literary way to emphasize the earthiness of a picture, as you will often see with wildlife or American Indian scenes or with land-scapes. Aesthetically the rough frame is appropriate on strong, rough-hewn work such as palette-knife paintings, for contrast to set off very smooth work, or to repeat rhythms or patterns con-tained or implied in the picture itself.

READY-MADE FRAMES

Nowadays we have a great advantage over past times in having a broad and varied choice of factory-produced items that save us money and the work of making them ourselves. This is as true in picture frames as it is in clothing, furniture, and every other item. Ready-made frames come in many styles and finishes and often are better and cheaper than we can make them ourselves, in styles ranging from the simplest 1/2-inch black to an elaborate Louis IV. They have the added advantage of being assembled and ready to try on like clothes, so that very little visualizing of the finished product is required. The most common standard sizes in inches are 5 by 7, 8 by 10, 9 by 12, 11 by 14, 12 by 16, 14 by 18, 16 by 20, 18 by 24, 20 by 24, 22 by 28, 24 by 30, 24 by 36, and 30 by 40, which are also standard sizes for glass and stretched canvas in the United States.

You should investigate the ready-made frame market in your area to see what is available. There are fine reproductions of styles from antiquity, contemporary inventions, and decorative frames, far more to choose from than ever before. In addition to the usual rectangular frame, there are ovals, rounds, and spandrels (rectangular-shaped frames with oval openings). Many frames come with liners (inserts), and these are made for oil or acrylic paintings, while most of the ones without liners are made for paperworks, to be used with mats. Ready-made frames are really quite versatile. You can "customize" them by changing the finish or color or by leafing them in part. Those frames that have liners are substantial woods, and by removing the liner, you can have an expensive-looking frame for a work on paper by adding a mat. (See Fig. 1-4.)

CUTTING A MAT

Mat cutting is a basic technique necessary to all framing of paperwork, and although it is possibly one of the most difficult skills to master in framing, perseverance and practice will gradually bring good, then excellent results. Because of the difficulty of doing it well with a mat knife, we recommend the Dexter mat cutter, which is still used by many professionals, but we are confident that there are and will be other equally good ones on the market.

PROPORTIONS

Throughout this book, in the area of aesthetics, we have attempted to avoid a rigid adherence to the fleeting taste or style of the times and present rules that are not dated and have a certain universality for all times. In some areas this is practically impossible, for prevailing tastes decide the modes of doing things in this and every other aspect of life. For instance, the fashion in the 1860s in Europe for framing drawings and etchings was to use a very wide mat and almost equally wide frame, as we can see in some of the interiors painted by the Impressionists. This style was prevalent even up to the end of World War I, having a great deal to do with the interior decor of the times, with its relatively heavy furniture and dark surroundings, which would have made a very delicate, small framework appear insignificant. In the 1930s the American Precisionists used relatively small mats and frames on their severely geometric renderings. Later with the invention of narrow metal-strip framing and the prevalence of expansive white walls in homes and museums, the wide mat made an appearance again, this time coupled with a very narrow frame, especially on modern abstract artwork. Sometimes there was no mat at all. The 1950s and 1960s seemed a time of extremes.

You should visit fine galleries and museums or look in decorator magazines to see what the prevailing styles are today. Your particular home furnishings and wall space are always cues to follow in making a framed picture effective in your home. Frames should be of a style consistent with your furniture or have at least some reference to something else in the room. If you have an expansive wall and are hanging only one picture, the framing must be substantial in size, keeping in mind, of course, the picture. When grouping a number of pictures, relatively smaller framing is usually best.

If we were to cite the single most important aspect of framing well, it would be in the area of proportion. Proportion of picture to mat, or of picture and mat or liner to frame is the one area that separates the true artistic framer from the mediocre or amateur one. Choices of color, value, size, and shape, however well selected, can be of little enhancement value if the proportions of these elements are ill chosen. The mat and frame combined make up the total frame for work on paper—photographs, drawings, watercolors, documents. Whether you decide upon a wide mat or a narrow one, its size and shape will determine the overall dimensions of the finished product. The mat, frame, and picture should cooperate gracefully in a size relationship to one another that is not boringly repetitious or ridiculously exaggerated in proportion. Generally there should be a size difference between mat and frame of at least an inch; when using a wide frame, use a narrow mat, and when using a narrow frame, use a wide mat. The forms in the picture itself will tell you how heavy the framing should be. Large or strong forms will call for heavier framing than delicately colored or rendered ones. Your mat and frame color will influence the overall size needed too, for dark-colored framing appears heavier than light-colored framing. Dark mats and colored ones usually look better when kept relatively small. If you wish to use an expansive mat, stick with a neutral light color, preferably white. Wide mats and narrow frames appear lighter in weight than wide frames and narrow mats. Small work, unless it is to hang in a large grouping or in a specific tiny wall space, should have wide framing; and conversely, the larger the work, the smaller the framing, relative to the picture.

A mat that is symmetrically distributed, that is, measures equally on all four sides, has a flattening effect, much as a flat panel frame has. This effect is entirely appropriate to flat-designed, non-perspective pictures, such as those of the primitives, the early Byzantine artists, or contemporary artists such as Josef Albers (see Fig. 1-6), but it is not often used on work with any depth or perspective. In most artwork, with the exceptions of those flat-designed pieces mentioned, there is a visual weight to the picture that makes a compensating larger bottom to the mat necessary for balance and support. Without the larger bottom, the mat appears smaller at the bottom or supporting edge, or the proportion may look "fat." In traditional perspective artwork on paper where a mat is required, a larger bottom of at least 1/2 inch (1.27 cm) is allowed, depending on size, on both vertical and horizontal pictures. On larger horizontal pictures, those over 20 by 24 inches (50 cm × 60 cm), a difference of 1 inch (2.5 cm) or more can make a pleasing proportion. On a strong horizontal picture with emphasis on the horizon or horizontal direction, sometimes larger size on the two sides can be an enhancement of the design, making the top a bit smaller than the sides, with the two ends of the picture the widest part of the mat. This is a relatively unusual proportion of the mat, but it is sometimes very effective in elongating the horizontal. Vertical pictures are often best presented in the well-known proportion of 3-inch (7.62-cm) sides, 4-inch (10.16-cm) top, and 5-inch (12.7-cm) bottom, emphasizing height. We find that a modification of these proportions, of differences of say 1/2 inch (1.27 cm) on a small work, lends a grace to the proportion.

In determining your proportion, analyze the composition of the picture. If it needs height, emphasize the vertical. If it needs width, add it. Note the proportions used in Figures 1-5, 1-6, and 1-7. In Figure 1-5, the basic composition is in a square format, since the bottom of the work is unfinished. To add size to the bottom would throw the design too far up in the frame; therefore, the mat is cut equally on all sides. Figure 1-6 is an all-square flat design, which naturally calls for a square-cut mat. The restful, heavy horizontal in Figure 1-7 needs extra support at the bottom to give it the most satisfying effect. Note in Figure 1-8 the unusual proportion of the mat. This is reminiscent of some of the fine Chinese procelain vases, which bulb up from the bottom and are abruptly shortened at the top, a uniquely Oriental idea. If you decide to use the wide frame—narrow mat idea, as you might well do on a reproduction of a painting or any work with big shapes, it is best to cut the mat

FIGURE 1-5. (left)
James J. Tissot: "Female
with Fur Scarf." Etching (1876). Private
collection, Jacksonville, Florida.

FIGURE 1-6. (below)
Josef Albers: "Homage
to the Square." Silk screen (1976).
Collection of the authors.

FIGURE 1-7,
Joseph Jeffers Dodge:
"Rocks near Rockport." Oil on
paper (1976). Collection of
Mr. and Mrs. Carle A. Felton, Jr.

FIGURE 1-8.
Torii Kiyonaga:
"Two Geisha Girls in a Precinct
of Ingri Shrine." Woodcut (around 1778).
Collection of the authors.

symmetrically and to have it perform a function similar to the liner in a frame for a painting, simply offering a "halo" inside the frame.

In order to help you visualize, at least approximately, the finished shape, it is very handy to have a corner sample of the frame—two mitered and joined lengths about 6 inches (15.24 cm) each—and either a mat corner sample or a piece of mat larger than you will need for the job. You can lay the picture on the mat and move the wooden corner sample around until you achieve a pleasing width relationship between picture, mat, and frame (Fig. 1-9a). While you are doing this, analyze the composition of the picture: If it is a vertical and seems to need height, accentuate it by adding length to the top and more to the bottom. If it has enough emphasis on the vertical direction in your judgment, do not add more. This is an eye-intuitive exercise. If the basic composition—the main lines and shapes that make up the picture—is square, stay with a square symmetrical mat. Add appropriate width to the bottom of any composition that seems to need added support.

FIGURE 1-9.
CUTTING A MAT.

FIGURE 1-9a.
Measure for the mat mechanically. Measure for the left side on the ruler, then count back from the right side to determine the width. For proportion, it may help to put the work on a larger piece of mat board and move it around, or to use a corner sample of mat board.

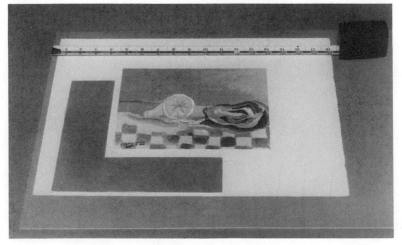

Diplomas are generally printed on rectangular horizontal papers, but the composition (the printing itself) is quite often in a square shape. To avoid a square appearance, keep the mat in a shape similar to the whole paper by not adding to the bottom nor coming in too close on the sides. Work that is crowded over the entire surface of the paper needs expanse of mat or panel for relief. A tiny image that is the center of interest in the page needs little or no matting. For results you can live with over the long term, it is best not to go to extremes or be too unconventional with mat shape. Practice and lots of looking will help develop a feeling for proportion. Some framers do say that it is better to make the mat too large than too small, so keep this in mind.

Another advantage in using a mat is that it can "crop" the picture to give it a better composition if need be. It allows leeway to center the work better or to "cut off" uninteresting or irrelevant parts. It should be mentioned also that in cutting a mat, you should allow room for all forms to be comfortably shown and not crowded by the mat. One example that comes to mind is a drawing we framed recently, which was composed of a large female figure whose body filled the sheet, with only half of the head showing at the top edge. We cut the mat wide enough at the top to allow room for the undrawn skull, so that the framing would be psychologically satisfying and she would not look like a woman with half a head.

SINGLE MATS

For cutting your own mats, you will need mat board and a mat-cutting tool, a large right angle or T square, a utility knife—all of which are available in art supply stores—and a smooth cutting surface, such as a plywood board covered with an extra piece of mat board.

Once your mat color and proportion have been decided upon, measure the outer dimensions of the mat size, keeping in mind how much of the mat will be covered by the lip of the frame. Draw out the shape of the outer mat with a T square, making certain that all corners are at perfect right angles. Cut out the basic mat shape with your cutting device following the straightedge. For this and other cutting, it may prove of invaluable assistance to place nails in the cutting board to steady your straightedge. There are many mat-cutting devices on the market for the home framer, but

FIGURE 1-9b.
The Dexter mat cutter, a hand-held
mat-cutting device.

of all of them the two least expensive and most practical are the
Dexter mat cutter and the ordinary utility knife or mat knife with a
comfortable handle.

The Dexter cutter (Fig. 1-9b) is a hand-held device with a blade
that can be adjusted to make an angle, or bevel, cut or a straight
perpendicular cut. It is more easily mastered than the knife, although making perfect cuts is always a process of learning and
takes much practice. To use the Dexter, you must cut from the
face (colored side) of the mat and push the cutter, using a
straightedge to guide. Its disadvantage is this front cutting, which
can scar the mat.

The utility, or mat, knife is more difficult to learn to control, especially
when cutting a uniform beveled edge, but has the advantage of
enabling you to cut mats from the back, which is very useful, as
you will see in our description of cutting a double mat.

After you have cut your basic mat shape, measure and mark all
four sides of the opening. Do all your measuring mechanically,
that is, using tape measure to determine basic size of the outer
mat and then widths of top, bottom, and sides, measuring in to the
desired opening of the cut mat. To figure out your measurements
mathematically can throw you into a state of confusion, especially
when making a subtle, precise measurement. Draw the opening
completely with lines overlapping when you are cutting from the
back with a knife. Place the straightedge along the drawn lines,
insert the mat knife tip approximately 1/8 inch (3.175 mm) beyond
the corner, and draw along the straightedge to 1/8 inch beyond
the next corner. Make a complete cut through the mat board the

first time, since repeating the cut will cause ragged edges. Experience will show you how far to cut beyond corner markings so that the corners will separate cleanly but not have overcuts.

In cutting with the Dexter, make only dots on the face of the mat at the four corners of the mat opening (Fig. 1-9c). Insert the blade directly into the first dot, then place your straightedge into position against the Dexter edge equally distant from the second dot. Push the cutter along the straightedge, holding the mat board and the straightedge firmly in place with your free hand (Fig. 1-9d). Use an emery board to sand off any ragged edges on the mat opening. fabric mat, a white to buff-colored cardboard is usually best, one

FIGURE 1-9c.
Mark the mat, face up, wtih dots to indicate corners of the opening.

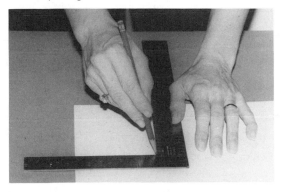

FIGURE 1-9d.
Cut the mat, using a T square, pushing the Dexter away from you.

37

DOUBLE MATS

It is of course logical to make a double mat using two boards of exactly the same size and cutting the inner mat 1/4 inch (6.3 mm) wider all around than the outer mat, then lining them up and gluing them together. But there is a way in which both boards can be cut very accurately in one piece, and this is a framer's trick that will ensure a perfectly uniform inner mat every time. To use it, you will have to cut the mats from the back.

First measure and cut the outer mat as instructed. Next, cut the shape of the inner mat, but don't cut its window yet. It can be a scrap any size that will adequately cover the opening of the outer mat. A size 1 inch (2.54 cm) smaller than the measurements of the outer mat will be ideal. Glue the inner mat, uncut, to the back of the outer mat; turn the joined mats over; place a dot of glue in the center of the cut opening, and replace the center of the cut opening into the outer mat. Weigh down this unit until dry. Next, turn the joined mats over and measure the opening to be cut, 1/4 inch (6.35 mm) or so larger than the outer mat, using the outer mat's edges to measure. Then cut as before, leaving the two mats glued together. Lift out the center and you have a perfect double mat without any lining up. You can use the centers for smaller mats or as backings.

With the Dexter cutter for a double mat you may also use a scrap as the inner mat by placing the cut outer mat on top of the inner mat, face up, and marking with a dot the diagonal of a square formed by placing a right angle 1/4 inch (6.35 mm) from each corner (Fig. 1-10), then cutting from dot to dot as before and gluing together afterward.

OVAL MATS

Cutting an oval mat freehand can be very tricky and will require a great deal of skill and ease in doing straight cuts first. Some very accomplished Dexter-cutter enthusiasts claim they can cut ovals of professional quality, needing only to sand off the place where the beginning and end of the cut meets. These cuts are made freehand following a pattern drawn on the mat.

It is easier to do small circular openings than it would appear, using a saucer, compass, or half dollar to draw the opening, then

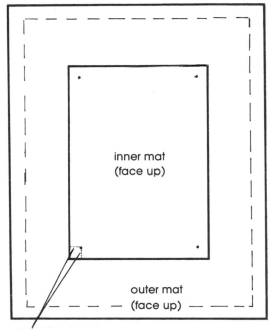

inner mat
(face up)

outer mat
(face up)

approx. 1/4 in.
(6.35 mm)

FIGURE 1-10.
In cutting a double mat with the Dexter, place the cut outer mat on top of the inner mat, which is a smaller piece, both face up. Mark the corner of the inner mat with a dot at the point formed by placing a right angle 1/4 inch (6.35 mm) on either side of the outer mat's corner, then cut and glue the mats together.

cutting carefully with a small mat knife. Some very nice decorative pictures can be done in this way.

COVERING MATS WITH FABRIC

Fine professional results can be achieved in framing by covering your mat with cloth, and it is easy to do. You may use burlap, linen, cotton, silk, or any other suitable material, keeping in mind the nature of the piece you are framing and the appropriate texture and color for the work's boldness or delicacy. Choose only fabrics that have a natural look—most synthetics are too regular and machine-made looking to be complementary in framing.

Elmer's glue is once again the framer's best choice for most fabrics, although with delicate fabrics, a spray glue is less likely to bleed through and make an ugly stain. To form the base of your with a smooth surface. Regular mat board is appropriate, or if you like the effect of a deeper bevel, you may use Fome-Cor.

After cutting the mat as described, cut a piece of fabric approximately 1 inch (2.54 cm) bigger all around than the mat. Watch the grain of fabric closely to ensure a professional look and be sure it has no creases and is ready to apply. Apply Elmer's uniformly with a brush all over the face of the mat, leaving no puddles (Fig 1-11a) and using only enough glue to make the fabric adhere. Test a

FIGURE 1-11.
COVERING THE MATS WITH FABRIC.

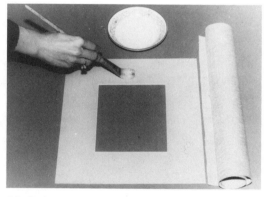

FIGURE 1-11a.
Coat the face of the mat with Elmer's glue.

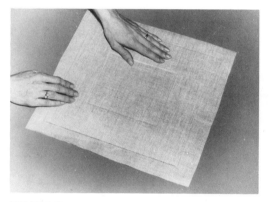

FIGURE 1-11b.
Place the fabric over the mat, smooth, and weigh down until dry.

FIGURE 1-11c.
Clip outer corners, center, and inner corners as shown, then glue into place on back side of mat.

FIGURE 1-11d.
Fabric-covered mat.

scrap of fabric to determine the amount of glue needed. On a large mat, you may use a 3- to 4-inch (approximately 10-cm) paint roller with a tray for the glue. You must work quickly, or the glue will dry in spots, causing bubbles in the fabric. Following the grain of the fabric carefully, line up the fabric over the mat board and press down, smoothing out perfectly and leaving no creases or bubbles. Weigh down under a flat surface until dry (Fig. 1-11b).

Cut the outer corners of the fabric as indicated in Figure 1-11c and cut out the center 1 inch (2.54 cm) from the opening of the mat. Clip the corners very close to the mat board—not too close, or the corner will look ragged, and not too far away, or the cloth will not turn under closely. Pull gently, and fold under, and glue the outside fabric edges, smoothing into place until dry; then do this with the inner "window" edges, making sure the corners are smoothly distinct (Fig. 1-11d)

MOUNTING PAPERS

The term MOUNT in picture framing generally means to secure the object to the backing so that it will be suspended and stay in place inside the frame. There are several different methods of mounting papers.

HINGING

A basic technique used in the mounting of all fine papers to be displayed in frames is to suspend the work on the backing by means of hinges. Hinges should be made of relatively thin paper, such as rice paper, the thickness dependent upon the weight or size of the paper to be framed. Rice paper can be bought in art supply stores by the single sheet, and if you are to be doing much framing or matting, you should familiarize yourself with what is available and experiment with different weights. You should purchase a jar of library paste from an office or school supply store. Remember that one sheet of rice paper and a jar of library paste will do innumerable pictures and will not stain them, so that these two materials are a very economical "must" to the framing of papers. To hinge the work, cut out or tear two or three pieces of rice paper, their size depending upon the weight of the paper to be held in place. For very lightweight pieces a size 1/2 inch by 1 inch (1.27 cm × 2.54 cm) is adequate. There are two methods of hinging described in Figure 1-12a. The first is done when the piece is to have a mat overlapping its edges. Center the piece on the backing and secure it there with a weight. Next, put glue on the part of the rice paper hinges that will hold the paper itself and place the hinges at the top corners of the back of the paper. Cut out or tear crosspieces of rice paper, glue them, and place them over the hinges to hold them in place on the backing. Weigh the hinges down until dry.

FIGURE 1-12.
TWO WAYS OF HINGING MATS.

FIGURE 1-12a.
Method of hinging when mat open will cover edges of artwork.

If the paper you are matting has nice edges or if you wish to expose the entire sheet with the mat opening not overlapping the edges, you will follow the other method of hinging shown in Figure 1-12b. This is called floating the picture. Center the paper on the backing as before. Fold the hinge in half, apply glue to front and back, and place the hinge at the top of the back of the paper as before, this time making it adhere to the paper and the backing at the same time. Weigh down these hinges until dry, then lift the paper and reinforce the hinge with a crosspiece of rice paper, weighing this down, too, until dry. Rice paper hinges that have been torn rather than cut tend to be less visible.

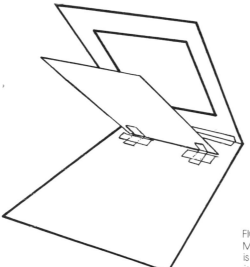

FIGURE 1-12b.
Method used when the entire paper
is to be exposed. This form of hinging
is known as floating the picture.

All "museum" or conservation mounting of papers is done by hinging.

WET MOUNTING

If you have an inexpensive print or poster to frame, the best results will be achieved in the final frame job by gluing it altogether to a stiff backing. There are a few glues available that have proven to be good for this purpose, and most of them are to be found in stores that carry wallpapers and their various pastes. New products are being put out every day, so you should experiment with them on various kinds of paper. The most widely used "tried and true" glue for papers in picture framing is wheat paste. This is available in powder form to be mixed with water and is particularly recommended because of its nonstaining, slow-drying, and fine adhering qualities. For the backing, you may purchase excellent mounting boards in art supply stores, but always use one of at least 1/8-inch (3.175-mm) thickness, preferably the kind with smooth white surfaces on both sides. Mounting "boards" are really made of paper.

First mix an ample amount of wheat paste to the consistency of cream, neither too thick nor too thin. The paste thickens more as exposed to the air. Next, cut the mounting board to a size larger than you will need, allowing room for the mat to rest on later. It is easier to cut down the backboard after the print has been mounted than to try to center it within a predetermined exact place. Draw a line around the picture to show its position on the mounting board. Cut a piece of brown paper or a paper similar in weight and size to the one you are mounting. This will serve as a "countermount" on the back of the mounting board to minimize buckling of the board.

With a sponge, wet the back of the paper picture you are to mount, being sure to wet it evenly all over, and carefully set it aside (Fig. 1-13a). Wet the brown paper in the same manner. Apply the wheat paste to the back of the mounting board quickly with a brush, then smooth the brown paper over it (Fig. 1-13b).

FIGURE 1-13.
WET MOUNTING.

FIGURE 1-13a.
Wet the back of the paper to be mounted and also another piece of paper of a similar size and weight to serve as a "countermount."

Apply glue to the front of the mounting board, making sure to evenly cover the entire area the picture is to occupy. Use only enough paste to do the job at hand. Lift the wet picture carefully and lower it, either at one end or in the middle, to the prepared paste area, then gently smooth or pat it down, making sure it is lined up correctly on the paste and that the paper's tensions are not going to cause creases or bubbles (Fig. 1-13c). A fairly wet paper will relax better and will smooth out well. If you see any bubbles, lift the paper and smooth it back down again until all bubbles are removed. With a rubber roller, bray all over to remove

FIGURE 1-13b.
Mount the "countermount" paper on the back of the mounting
board with wheat paste.

any remaining air pockets, from the center outward, then weigh
down under glass overnight. The next day remove the glass, lay
the piece on a flat surface and let dry for several days.

If you are mounting a watercolor or a heavy paper, you may
apply the wheat paste directly to the back of the paper to wet
and relax it and then place it on the mounting board in the same
manner. Do not be overly frightened about wetting papers. Re-

FIGURE 1-13c.
Spread wheat paste on board and mount the artwork, smoothing from center
outward to remove air bubbles. Weigh down until dry.

member, they are made from wet pulp, and when they are to be mounted, they are not hurt by being wet first, provided the wetting is uniform. However, they should be handled carefully to prevent tearing or damage to the image. Thin papers such as rice paper and light-bodied papers with water-soluble color should not be wet-mounted.

DRY MOUNTING

Most mounting by professional framers is done in a dry-mount press, which is the equivalent of a huge iron, heated to an appropriate temperature and applied to the paper, which rests on an adhesive sheet on the mounting board, and pressed until the paper and adhesive adhere to the board. These dry-mount adhesive sheets are available in some art supply stores on the retail level and can be used at home with a regular iron. There are spray adhesives of this iron-on type too. Check in your area to find out what is available to you. Dry mounting is particularly effective for photographs and lighter-weight papers.

For pictures that are not over 16 inches by 20 inches (approximately 40 cm × 50 cm), there are adhesive sheets on the market called cold-mount sheets. With these, the picture is smoothed into place with the use of a squeegee. Various spray mounts in spray cans are more widely available and are useful in mounting small, thin, or porous absorbent papers, but are risky because of their uneven drying and the inability to reposition or correct faults in laying down the paper the first time. They are entirely unsuitable for mounting anything large.

ASSEMBLING THE MAT, WORK, AND BACKING.
THE BACKING

To frame a picture on paper, you must use a backing to hold the picture in place inside the mat. This is separate from the final or outer backing, and is the surface the picture rests on, whether hinged or permanently mounted. Even if you are using no mat, you will still need a backing.

The backing could be any rigid surface, from a piece of paper with body to a wooden board (as was used in earlier times, but without present knowledge of good framing conservation practices). We would urge you to use those backings that have low acidity, lower relative to the value of what you are framing. As we have stated, the cheapest paper boards, such as corrugated board and cardboard have the most acid or impurity content, and better paper boards have less—100 percent rag museum board and the newer substitutes for this having the least. We would suggest that the backing be mat board, mounting board, or illustration board on less valuable pieces, watercolor paper or other rag-content rigid paper on somewhat more valuable pieces, and museum board or its equivalent on very valuable ones.

Corrugated board or Fome-Cor can then be used as an outer stiff backing.

TWO METHODS OF MATTING

After you have determined the size and shape of your mat and have cut its opening, cut the backing the same size. If you are hinging the artwork into place, tape the top of the mat inside to the top of the backing (Fig. 1-14a). Fold into a booklike form and line up the mat with the backing. Press down the taped edge to secure well. Open the mat and insert the picture, lining up the picture properly with the opening. When the picture is in place, put

FIGURE 1-14.
ASSEMBLING THE MAT, WORK, AND BACKING.

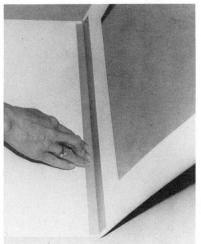

FIGURE 1-14a.
Tape the mat to the backing at the inside top. Fold together and line up.

FIGURE 1-14b.
Center the artwork in the mat and weigh down temporarily.

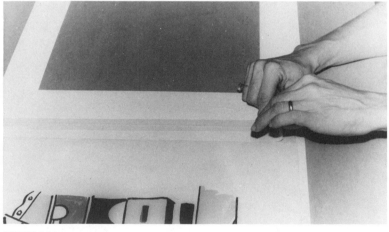

FIGURE 1-14c.
Hinge the artwork into place.

a weight on it, open the mat, and hinge the picture into place (Fig. 1-14b). When this has been accomplished, the piece is matted (Fig. 1-14c). To mat a mounted picture, glue with Elmer's all around the picture itself on the backing, then put the mat in place and weigh down until dry. Trim the backing edges afterward.

For museum matting, use four-ply museum board for both mat and backing. Tape the top of the mat as shown in Figure 1-14, and hinge the picture with rice paper and library paste.

SELECTING GLASS
REGULAR GLASS

Single-strength clear window glass is the old standby in the framing of papers and is, with the need for the protection of glass at all, still the best. Once you have looked a great deal at pictures, you may come to a realization that glass after all has a nice unifying effect between the mat and the picture, indeed, between the colors in the picture itself, just as the final varnish on an oil painting has a unifying effect on all the pigments used. In some cases glass can bring the picture into unity with a shiny frame, such as a chrome or metal-leaf frame, making the work and frame a more integrated object.

Clear glass should be used on watercolors or their reproductions to accent the sparkling, crisp quality of the medium; on etchings and fine line drawings in ink or pencil for clarity; and for subtle toned work where a clear view is needed. In general it should be used on all original work and most artwork. All museums and fine art collectors use clear glass or clear Plexiglas on their works on paper.

NONGLARE GLASS

Nonglare glass is glass with a light-diffusing chemically-etched surface that eliminates the reflective characteristic of clear glass and is commonly considered to look like no glass at all. This, as well as the theory that nonglare glass has properties of protecting the work from ultraviolet rays, is a misconception. By holding it up and looking through it, one cannot see anything at a distance through nonglare glass. To demonstrate this to yourself, ask your glass company to show you samples of each kind of glass. In the framing of your artwork, be careful in the choosing of nonglare glass. Although it looks very well on some photographs and printed matter such as diplomas, nonglare glass does tend to dull the colors and to distort the image from different angles of view. Its real use is depicted in its name: In rooms with lots of sunlight, or even in dark rooms with artificial lights, artwork under clear glass is disturbingly difficult to see, especially work with black or a very dark background, and this is where nonglare glass should be considered.

PLEXIGLAS

Plexiglas is really clear acrylic in sheet form. It is becoming more and more commonly used in every phase of our lives. In contemporary picture framing with the no-frame idea prevailing, it is replacing not only the glass but also the frame itself. Unlike glass it has practically no tendency to bond with paint or paper, so that many framers use it directly in contact with the artwork or photograph without the intervening mat. We have read that it has far less moisture buildup through condensation as well. It comes in various thicknesses and is lighter weight than glass. Its resistance to breakage lends it well to travel in our transient society, and traveling exhibitions of museums use it commonly.

Plexiglas is available in clear form, but also in nonglare and in a special form with an ultraviolet filter, which can help protect artwork for a time from light damage. Its major drawback is its vulnerability to scratching, thus it must always be cleaned with a very soft cloth. We feel that as it is developed and perfected more and more, it will be used increasingly in framing.

CUTTING GLASS

Glass can be purchased by the single sheet or by the box in the standard sizes mentioned in the section on ready-made frames. For unusual sizes, some glass companies will cut your glass to order, charging only for the size you use. However, it is easy to cut glass yourself with a simple metal-wheel glass cutter and a

FIGURE 1-15.CUTTING GLASS.

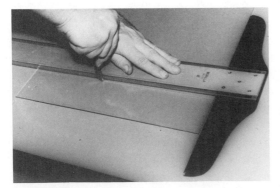

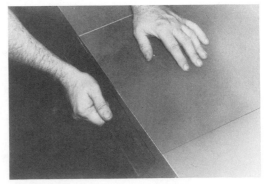

FIGURE 1-15a.
Measure and score the glass with a glass cutter and T square. A correct score has been made when you hear an even scratch sound.

FIGURE 1-15b.
Break the glass from the edge of the table with a snap.

straightedge, on a flat table with a right-angle side or a plywood board to support and break the glass.

Mark off your measurements with a felt-tip pen, making your glass 1/8 inch (3.175 mm) smaller than the frame opening from rabbet to rabbet length and width. Line up the straightedge and score the glass with one stroke, bearing down firmly while holding the cutter at an even right angle to the glass for the entire score (Fig. 1-15a). Follow the straightedge carefully—you needn't make a fast stroke, but concentrate on even pressure and straight line. Speed will come with practice. The proper score is made when you hear an even scratch sound. Do not score more than once, or you will ruin the cutter. Move the glass to the edge of the table even with the scored line and, holding the remaining glass firmly down on the table with one hand and center of the glass to be cut off with the other, push firmly and quickly with a snap to break off at the score. (Fig 1 15b).

For small pieces of glass, tap the underside of the score at one end with the metal ball of the cutter to start the score breakage, then place the score line over a pencil at this end and press down on both sides of the glass.

MAKING FRAMES

You are in for a surprise if you have never made a frame before. There is something genuinely thrilling about seeing this familiar object come into being under your own hands, especially if you are making it from raw lumberyard wood in a design you've thought up yourself.

To ensure the best results and not to waste effort and funds, you will have to do some careful planning ahead of time. First you will need some equipment and preferably a place to work where you are not concerned about a mess and can set up shop in a relatively permanent manner. If you have a place for a freestanding sturdy workbench accessible from all sides, this is the ideal. You will need some form of mitering device to cut the molding at 45-degree angles and a vise to hold the mitered pieces in place while gluing and nailing them. People who are accustomed to working with wood can adapt their woodworking tools to frame making without the use of special equipment; for instance, a woodworker can draw out a 45-degree angle (the necessary angle cut to make a mitered corner) using a combination square and cut the corner freehand with a saw, then join the miter using a common bench vise, holding the free side in place while nailing. But here we demonstrate using a miter box and miter vise, tools made especially for this purpose, which we think make it easier. You should tailor the quality of your equipment to suit your budget, remembering that better equipment will bring better results and hold up longer, but that it is silly to invest a lot unless you plan to do much framing. The miter box we show here is very economical. It is made by Durall-Eagle and has a built-in miter vise; we have coupled it with a Stanley saw of 13 points to the inch. If you are going to do much framing, invest in a good miter box, miter vise, and fine-toothed saw.

Your miter box and your vise should both be screwed to the workbench at convenient places, with the vise at one corner for easy access. Another permanent installation is a strip of wood nailed to one end of the bench to brace the completed frame against when you are nailing the picture in, so that you will not knock the frame corners apart (see Fig. 1-21b). You will need a hammer, a drill, brads of all sizes, a nail set to sink the brads, a measuring tape or ruler, and carpenter's glue. Incidentally, many areas have community school systems with facilities and classes in woodworking where equipment is available. You might look into this and try your hand at frame making before setting up shop at home—it will give you a chance to get the feel of wood construction and perhaps some invaluable tips about joining and equipment. No one is more knowledgeable in this field than a veteran woodworker, and hopefully your instructor or classmate might be one.

You need to use a little common sense about construction to design and make a frame from raw wood molding. You need to plan ahead carefully, knowing exactly, step by step, what procedure you will follow in constructing it. It is disheartening to put time and work into a project that proves to be impracticable or impossible, or to find, after all your hours of work, that you have used the wrong kind of wood or an unbecoming frame style for your picture. Keep in mind the basic requirements of the picture frame (see Fig. 1-16) and visit your lumber supply house to find out exactly what is available to you. Many lumberyards will give you small samples (see Fig. 1-19), which you can practice combining in various ways to come up with a style appropriate for your picture. Plan the frame all the way to completion, including its finish. If you are going to leave a natural- or stained-wood finish, buy a piece of lumber that has an attractive grain or no grain—white pine, ponderosa pine, and basswood are good for this. More expensive hardwoods, such as walnut or maple, should be used only when you are really knowledgeable and sure of yourself. Imagine, after all your work, finding that the wood has a zebra-stripe appearance or an unsightly blemish in the grain when you have planned a natural- or stained-wood finish. Experience will be your best teacher, and we hope that we can help keep you from making too many mistakes as you venture into this wonderful handicraft.

CHOOSING UNFINISHED MOLDINGS

Two molding types used for picture frames are prerabbeted picture frame molding and unrabbeted house trim and furniture trim molding, both of which come in linear footage lengths. Figure 1-16

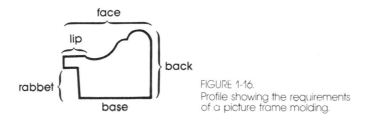

FIGURE 1-16.
Profile showing the requirements
of a picture frame molding.

shows the basic profile requirements for the picture frame. A rabbet is a cut made in the molding to keep the picture from falling out. Regardless of molding shape, you must have, or create, a rabbet to hold the picture in the frame.

To save time and for convenience, most professionals use finished, rabbeted moldings to make their frames. Naturally this is easier and requires less ingenuity than using unfinished builders' molding, but finished frame moldings are not always available to the non-professional, and certainly not in the great variety that is possible by combining the house-trim types in different ways. We have selected some common profiles that are adaptable to the making of picture frames when combined to create a rabbet (Fig. 1-17). You must check with your own builders' molding suppliers to see what is available to you and then work out your own combi-

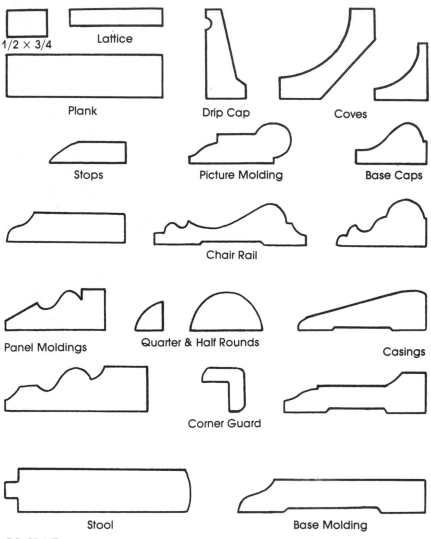

1/2 × 3/4   Lattice

Plank   Drip Cap   Coves

Stops   Picture Molding   Base Caps

Chair Rail

Panel Moldings   Quarter & Half Rounds   Casings

Corner Guard

Stool   Base Molding

FIGURE 1-17.
Profiles of common builders' moldings that could be used to make picture frames.

nations to form the kind of frame you will need for the particular job at hand.

Always choose moldings that have a flat surface which will serve as the base of the frame. Rounded- or slanted-bottom moldings cannot be cut properly in the miter box, nor joined in the miter vise. Some cove moldings, which make scoop frames, must be selected with this in mind, since they are the most difficult to work with and must be joined in the vise upside down in order to clamp them into place.

The most common frame styles are reproduced in Figure 1-18, but you should experiment on your own to find practical, workable frames that resemble these. Here we demonstrate one simple combination to form a basic frame style (Fig. 1-19). You may experiment broadly with different possibilities, but it may prove most successful to keep these basic shapes in mind. If you have a router or table saw with which to cut your own rabbet or access to a millwork shop to do it for you, you will be saved the step of rabbet making with two moldings and need only be concerned with style and finish.

FIGURE 1-18.
Profiles of common picture frame moldings.

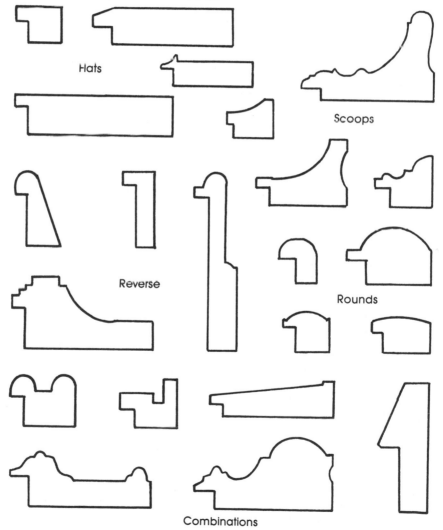

Flats

Scoops

Reverse

Rounds

Combinations

Many books on the subject of wood finishing have been written, and we do not have space here to elaborate in great depth, but we do offer guidelines for suitable picture frame finishes. There are natural, waxed, unfinished woods and varnished, painted, and stained ones; there are wire-brushed rustic finishes and smooth metal-leaf ones, and all the combinations of these. Primary considerations for the finishing of any raw wood are the following: (a) for natural wood finish, use wood sealer, then clear or spar varnish; (b) for stained wood, use stain, then varnish to seal; (c) for a painted surface (enamel or latex), use paint primer, then paint.

You should experiment with scrap pieces of wood first to obtain the kind of finish you wish to achieve, and remember that each wood has its own character and takes differently to different finishes. Since most builders' moldings are made from relatively soft woods such as fir, basswood, and pine, you must take care in finishing, especially in staining. Varnish and shellac each give different colors to various woods. The finish we have found to influence natural wood appearance least is a clear acrylic coating of gloss or matte medium, used by artists and found in art supply stores, which is steel-wooled when dry and then given a coat of hard wax such as carnauba, which is found under such brand names as Simonize. Finishes of this kind should be used only on very attractive natural wood.

The most often recommended paint for frames is casein, known by brand names like Luminall in paint stores. Enamel in spray form can be used for decorator frames. More subtle color may be added to your frame by using an antiquing kit. For texture or ground you may use several coats of artist's gesso tinted with earth-color acrylic paints such as yellow ochre and raw umber, sanding the final coat with fine sandpaper or scratching into it to obtain a rough texture. Some of the nicest finishes for frames are achieved by alternating two or three layers of different color, then sandpapering to bring out hints of the separate colors. When using this process, be sure to isolate each layer with varnish, allowing every step to dry thoroughly before proceeding with the next. The final layer will set the tone of the frame and should be a relatively neutral one. Chemically speaking, oil- and water-base colors cannot be mixed, but you can use them both in this process if you remember to use the waterbase ones underneath—

"fat over lean," as they say. Once the final sanding is done, you may use a varnish tinted slightly with stain to unify the whole finish. You may then spatter fly specks using dark wet paint on a toothbrush.

Although leafing is a skill that requires much practice, gold and silver metal-leaf kits can be fun to experiment with, following the instructions included in the kit. Your best results here will be in using it to trim rather rustic frames, without concern about complete smoothness.

CUTTING AND JOINING THE MOLDING

Here we have selected a basic platform frame style, created with the use of a 1-inch (2.54-cm) half round, a 1/2-inch by 3/4-inch (1.27-cm × 1.905-cm) flat, or parting, bead, and a plank 3/4-inches by 2-3/4 inches (1.9 cm × 7 cm) (see Fig. 1-19).

FIGURE 1-19.
From these three builders' moldings we shall construct a frame.

First the picture is measured for length and width (Fig. 1-20a). Do this and all measuring with extreme accuracy, allowing in this case 1/8 inch (3.175 mm) larger than these measurements for ease of admitting the picture into the finished frame. We are creating the rabbet with the plank and parting bead, with the half round on top to make the lip, so the plank and parting bead will be our guiding measurements, therefore cut first. Cut one side of the plank to a 45-degree angle, measure off the needed width for the picture, and cut the other side. Always remember that the inner side of the frame (the side facing away from you in the miter box) is the place the picture is to fit in (Fig 1-20b). When you have cut all four plank pieces, which form the base of your frame, measure and mark the parting bead to fit the inner edge of the plank (Fig. 1-20c) and cut all four of these pieces. This is the second part of the frame's rabbet to rest on top of the plank frame and to raise the half round (which will form the lip) from the plank. Finally measure and cut the half round with its outer edge exactly to fit the outer edge of the parting bead. When these two parts are joined together later, they will create the lip of the rabbet (see Fig. 1-16).

Now you are ready to construct. Sand the mitered corners to smooth them and prepare them for the glue. Glue works best on smooth surfaces, and it is really the glue and not the nails which holds your frame together. Many of our modern glues are so strong that nails aren't even necessary—and you can actually make a frame without the use of a vise or nails, by simply gluing the corners and clamping them until they are dry. Apply glue to the plank miter (Fig. 1-20d), line up one short end and one long end of the plank frame in the vise, clamp, and let dry for several minutes, the longer the better. Drill in two places for the nails to

FIGURE 1-20.
CUTTING AND JOINING THE MOLDING.

FIGURE 1-20a.
Measure the artwork or width of the desired frame opening.

FIGURE 1-20b.
Measure and cut the plank one corner at a time, from first inner corner cut to second inner corner cut, equal to the artwork's dimensions, plus a small allowance, say 1/8 inch (3.175 mm).

FIGURE 1-20c.
Measure the parting bead to fit the inner plank size, then cut as before. Cut the half round with its outer edge the size of the outer parting bead. This piece will form the lip of the rabbet.

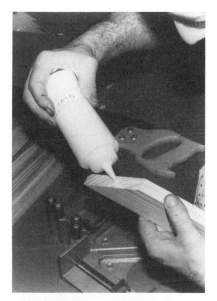

FIGURE 1-20d.
Use carpenter's glue when joining.

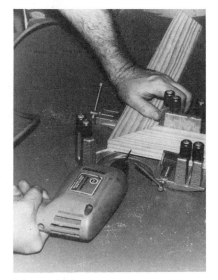

FIGURE 1-20e.
Tighten in the vise, placing the corner perfectly. Drill first to place the nails.

FIGURE 1-20f.
Nail with brads of adequate size, then let the corner glue dry in the vise. Repeat this procedure with the parting bead frame.

enter (Fig. 1-20e) and then nail (Fig. 1-20f). Repeat with the other short and long pieces to form two L's, then join the two L's in the same way. The fourth corner is always the hardest, and extremely accurate measuring and cutting is the only way the frame will come together perfectly. Join the parting bead into a frame similarly, then the half round, using only glue (Fig. 1-20g). When you have made all three frames (Fig. 1-20h), join them together as illustrated (Figs. 1-20i and 1-20j), using glue and then nails. To finish this frame, we painted the platform a decorative color to suit the picture's subject and left the rounded front a natural color, so we finished the parts separately before putting the whole frame together. If there are slightly open corners, use plastic wood to fill them and the nail holes formed after the nails are driven below the surface, then sand before finishing.

FIGURE 1-20g.
Gluing is adequate with some frames. Join half rounds this way, letting the glue dry.

FIGURE 1-20h.
When all three frames are joined, you are ready to put them together.

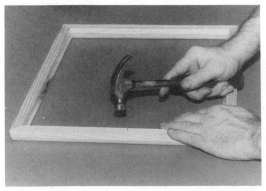

FIGURE 1-20i.
Nail the parting bead to the half round from the bottom as shown.

FIGURE 1-20j.
Nail the plank to the top frame. And you have a platform frame, made from lumberyard wood.

FITTING THE WORK INTO THE FRAME

Now that you have chosen your materials, matted your work, made your frame, and cut your glass, all that remains is to put them together. This is known in framer's terms as fitting.

Cut a final stiff backing of corrugated board or Fome-Cor, and a piece of brown paper somewhat larger than the outer frame size. Place the frame face down on a soft surface such as a blanket or towel to prevent damage. Insert the glass and clean thoroughly with glass cleaner and paper towels. With a paintbrush remove any lint or debris (Fig. 1-21a). Brush the mat to be sure it has no spots, then insert the matted picture and final backing into frame. Check by turning the frame on its side for any remaining spots inside the glass. If it is clean, secure the picture into the frame with small brads and a tack hammer, bracing the frame against a backboard (Fig. 1-21b). If you are using a delicate frame or framing a work such as a pastel, or if you are working with an object mounted in a shadow box, you should use a pair of pliers, padded as shown, to squeeze the brads in (Fig. 1-21c).

Be sure the mat is well centered in the frame. You can still adjust it with a screwdriver edge inserted at the seam if necessary. Tape the seams with masking tape to seal the work well. With Elmer's glue, make a line all around the frame's back edge and smooth

FIGURE 1-21. FITTING THE WORK INTO THE FRAME.

FIGURE 1-21a.
Clean the glass and brush out all dust spots, then insert the artwork and stiff backing.

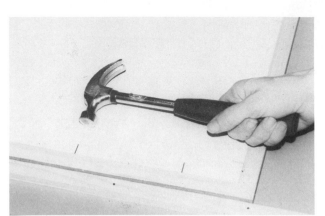

FIGURE 1-21b.
Place the frame against a backboard and tack the picture in
with brads.

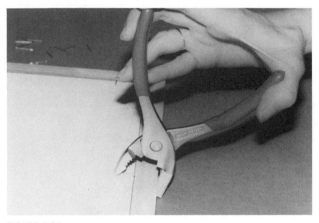

FIGURE 1-21c.
Or you may squeeze the brads in with a padded pair of pliers.

FIGURE 1-21d.
Tape the edges of the backing to the frame to seal, then apply
a line of Elmer's glue all around the back of the frame.

FIGURE 1-21e.
Put brown paper on the back, then trim with a razor blade.

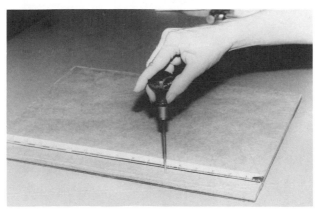

FIGURE 1-21f.
Measure for the screw eyes, then make holes with an awl.

with the finger (Fig. 1-21d). Place brown paper over the back and smooth it down over the edges. With a single-edge razor, trim the paper, using your middle finger to guide along the side of the frame (Fig. 1-21e). Smooth all the edges firmly and clean up the excess glue. With a sponge, dampen the paper backing and allow to dry. This will shrink your "dust cover" and make it tight as a drum. To place the screw eyes, measure approximately one-quarter to one-third of the way down the sides of the frame, and make holes with an ice pick or awl (available in hardware stores) (Fig. 1-21f). Put the screw eyes into place, then wire. Judge by weight the sizes you will need and be careful not to use too lightweight a wire for the job at hand.

WORKS
ON CLOTH

2

Works on cloth are oil and acrylic paintings on canvas, needleworks of all kinds, and any other work done on fabric backings. They are, with few exceptions, stretched on appropriate stretching devices and put into frames without mats or glass.

FIGURE 2-1.
Cross-stitch sampler. Worked by Emma Moss.
Lent by Janet Hall.

OIL AND ACRYLIC PAINTINGS ON CANVAS

In the past, the painting was considered to be the masterwork of the artist. More valuable, more highly prized than any preliminary sketches or drawings, it was the culmination of the artist's know-how and creativity, and, unlike the sketches, which were kept in folios, it was the piece that was intended to be hung. Paintings have a built-in permanence of their own and therefore need very little preparation for framing beyond stretching. The chemistry of the materials—the primed cotton or linen canvas, the nonfugitive colors, and the final varnish—is made to last.

STRETCHING CANVAS

The stretching of both painted and unpainted canvas is the same: You must determine the measurements and purchase two stretcher strips for the length and two for the width from an art supply store. Stretcher strips are sturdy, kiln-dried wooden bars with slots for joining, especially designed to form the frame for stretching canvas or heavy cloth, and are sold by linear-inch lengths only. Since canvas is to be stretched so tightly and has a good amount of pliability, canvas pliers are almost a must, and you will need a staplegun or carpet tacks and hammer. If you are working with a canvas that has been stretched previously and has been trimmed around the edges, you will have to sew 1-1/2-inch (3.8-cm) strips of canvas to each of the four edges for something to hold on to while stretching. (See Fig. 2-5.)

Join each length and width of stretcher strips to form an L, then join the two L's together to form the stretcher frame, making certain the corners fit, using a right-angle device to be certain they are square (Fig. 2-2a). Center the canvas over the stretcher frame and tack down the center of one length. Use two or three tacks at intervals of, say 2-1/2 inches (6.35 cm). Turn to the opposite side and, pulling so that the center is taut, tack again two or three times (Fig. 2-2b). Repeat this center-tacking on the two shorter sides. Once you have secured all the centers, gradually continue to tack from the centers toward the corners, alternating between opposite sides, always keeping the tensions equal, until all sides are secure and only the corners remain. Secure the corners as illustrated in Figure 2-2c.

FIGURE 2-2.
STRETCHING CANVAS.

FIGURE 2-2a.
Put stretcher strips together tightly and at perfect right angles.

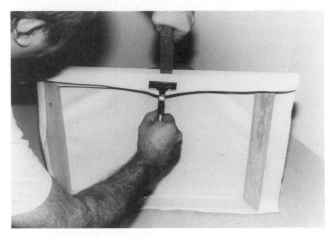

FIGURE 2-2b.
Staple centers first, then sides, using canvas pliers.

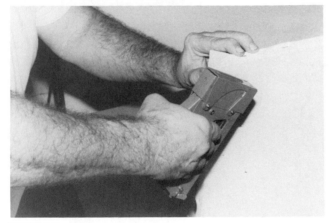

FIGURE 2-2c. Finish corners as shown.

Because canvases may have to be restretched in time, we recommend leaving at least an inch (2.54 cm) of border all around and stapling it to the back of the stretcher frame.

PROPER FRAMES

We are conditioned to expect paintings to be framed in certain ways, although of course styles have changed through the centuries. In recent history many museums and fine galleries have begun to frame their artworks in frames of the particular period of the work. Many modern works have been framed in simple strips or no frame at all.

We have already discussed basic guidelines for molding shapes and their use in the section on paper (see page 23)—angular or flat on straight-line or flat design, round or scoop on curvilinear or perspective design. With paintings, the frame's size, shape, and color are all-important; since there is not the intervening enhancement and width of the mat, the frame is everything.

In the distant past, since the earliest use of the frame as we know it, the frame was designed and built for the particular painting by the artist or artisan, who was commissioned and paid by the Church or a wealthy patron. With today's manufacturing system a wide variety of relatively economical ready-made frames are on the market, from very elaborate styles to simple stripping. You should probably consider a ready-made if you are framing a painting, for the variety of style and the price are hard to beat and there is no visualizing or surprise in the finished product, since you can try it on the painting just as you try on clothes. If you do decide to make your own frame from scratch, follow the needs of the painting for size, style, and finish.

You will need to rely on your eyes for guidance in choosing the proper frame for a painting, always having in mind where it is to hang, with what furnishings and surrounding matter. Many homes today combine period furnishings using many different styles, and if this is true in your case, you may simply choose whatever you would consider to be the best frame for the painting (which ideally is what should be done anyway). Other homes have period furnishings, which dictate to a certain extent what frame can be used; in that case you will have to strike a delicate balance between enhancement of the work and suitability for the room. Usually this can be accomplished by following the guidelines set forth in Chapter 1 for proper shape, size and color, with necessary modifications for the room's sake, unless the painting itself is utterly incongruous with the decor.

One rule in choosing frames for paintings has been: The smaller the painting, the larger the frame, and the larger the painting, the smaller the frame, in proportion (see Fig. 4-1). Paintings require more substantial frames than do works on paper because of the heavier character of the medium, the thickness of the stretcher strips, and the more traditional presentation. Even paintings on panels that could conveniently be accommodated by small frames seem to require larger ones to be psychologically satisfying.

All pictures have a visual weight. Aside from the subject matter, a small painting with heavy impasto or dark or bright colors may weigh more visually than a larger one with delicate tones and forms or vast misty areas, as in Oriental landscapes. Frames also have visual weight apart from size or actual physical weight. A small heavily carved dark frame can weigh more visually than a delicately ornamented pale-colored frame twice its size. A simple molding seems to be less weighty than an ornate one of the same size and color.

When looking at a frame for your painting, consider the following points:

- Is the frame the proper weight? Is it strong enough visually to contain the forms adequately? Active, moving forms or predominating diagonal lines in the painting's design will require a heavy frame visually to hold them in place, as will large, colorful, or heavily painted forms. Delicate colors and small forms or restful horizontal compositions require more delicately colored and carved, or simpler, frames.

- Is the shape correct for the work? Remember, scoop frames emphasize perspective and are therefore suitable for three-dimensional pictures; they suggest intimacy and are good for interior scenes, flower arrangements, and portraits. Reverse and flat frames emphasize flatness, lending themselves to flat, nonperspective work such as that of the primitive painters and modern abstractionists.

- Are the color and ornament (or lack of it) enhancing to the piece? The frame's color should "pick up" the general tone of the painting or contrast with it enhancingly. Ornaments, whether delicate or high-relief, and overall shape should echo forms in the painting and serve as further repetition of forms rather than introduce forms foreign to the work.

A knowledge of the history of frames is very helpful here in order to know the various styles of painting in the past and what was used as framing. You may achieve great visual training by visiting museums and galleries, observing not only the framing of the picture itself but, in some of the genre paintings of interiors, framed pictures of the day on the walls.

It is an interesting postulate that early people may have chosen to position themselves on certain spots, perhaps on hills, from which they could contemplate the beauties of the land by peering through foliage that "framed" a particularly lovely view. Modern photographers are instructed to shoot scenes of landscape with "framing" foreground foliage in order to reference their works and put them into perspective. Since early times the frame has evolved with much this same theme. Early frames were adorned with leaf forms, sometimes vinelike, all around the picture. Many of them were like doorways or portals with ivy adornment to soften and present rhythmic relief to the hard architectural forms. When intellectual ideas pervaded—in the late eighteenth century, for example—forms hardened to geometric adaptations of the earlier flowing plant forms.

You will notice in museums that most of the old masterworks are framed in gold. Gold has had the significance of being eternal through the ages. It has been used in paintings and in ornamentation for centuries with this significance, and we use it similarly for wedding rings. The religious subjects we have inherited from our predecessors have traditionally been ornamented with gold. And so, when choosing the frame for an important work, gold might be our first thought. Another interesting historic fact is that in the late 1860s, when the Impressionists took their easels out of the studio and did their colorful paintings of the effects of light, they also rebelled against the gilded frame of their predecessors and painted the frames white to offset their works.

In our own truly contemporary styles of painting, many artists design their works to be entities in themselves, with little or no frame at all, and if you own one of these works, it is best not to contradict the artist's wishes by imposing more frame than is called for. Other popular paintings today range in style and subject matter from old barns and wildlife to flat abstractions. Commercial frames are available that reflect these themes and should be chosen according, with the general rules of good framing in mind.

LINERS

In picture framing, the wooden insert in the frame opening that separates the painting from the molding is known as the liner. Liners can be cloth-covered, painted, or finished in the same manner as the frame, and perform a function similar to that of the mat in the framing of papers, providing an enhancing relief between picture and frame. Liners have come into vogue only since the early 1900s, so they are a relatively late development of the frame. Many museums have used them to adjust sizes in the attempt to match paintings with appropriate frames of their period.

Liners can be covered with any fabric, such as gingham (see Fig. 2-11), linen, burlap, suede, or velvet, so long as it is a fabric that is suitable for the painting. To make a liner, you must locate a molding in a shape that will fit under the lip of the outer frame to form a smooth, uncomplicated border around the picture. One possibility using a combination of two builders' moldings would be a 1-inch (2.54-cm) stop and a 1/2-inch by 3/4-inch (1.27-cm × 1.9-cm) parting bead (see Fig. 1-17), which would be put together in a manner similar to that in Figure 1-20, replacing the half round with the stop molding. After cutting and joining the two frames together to form the liner, cover the stop with strips of linen or other cloth using Elmer's glue, then carefully razor-blade the cloth to fit at the corners. After this, you are ready to build the outer frame, using the liner's measurements (see Fig. 2-1).

FITTING THE CANVAS INTO THE FRAME

To assemble stretched canvas and frame, you may place the canvas into the frame and, with approximately 1-inch (2.54-cm) brads, angle through the stretcher strips and hammer into the frame. Or you may use Clip-its, spring clips, or mirror holders, as shown in Figure 2-3, which cause less damage to painting, stretcher strips and frame, and facilitate removal.

BACKINGS

Canvas, like all cloth, needs a maximum of air circulation for its long-term preservation; therefore, a total lack of backing really is

FIGURE 2-3.
Fitting the canvas into the frame. Use Clip-its or other clips as shown.

best. If your environment is exceptionally dusty, you may use a backing on your painting that has many air holes, such as pegboard cut to the size of the back of your canvas or frame, or use a paper board backing with holes cut in, glued only on the four corners of the frame or stretcher strips.

NEEDLEWORK: BASIC PREPARATION

Aesthetically, it is our present-day feeling that it is best to work with nature and not to force anything into an artificial form. This is true in the framing of needlework, and it is one reason for not using glass over it. When you use glass, with or without mats, much of the tactile quality of stitchery is lost, and the piece looks more like a print. Since cloth has body and is not easily torn, it cooperates perfectly with being stretched to a firm tightness on a stretcher frame, which gives it the best appearance without wrinkles and shows off the handwork.

Many experts tell us that glass should not be used in the framing of cloth pieces because they need air circulation for their preservation; cloth "breathes," as they say. Glass can have moisture build-up inside through condensation under changing weather conditions, and that will create favorable conditions for mildew and other fungi. There are cases, however, when glass is warranted, when the environment presents more of a hazard than does glass, such as in the kitchen. In these cases the glass should be removed from the cloth in a shadow box technique. (We discuss this aspect of framing in Chapter 3.)

STRETCHING NEEDLEWORK

For stretching needlework you will need a staplegun. The best would be one for general household use, because the staples are thinner and have less tendency to cause runs in the fabric than the heavy-duty kind. The stretcher frame is what holds your needlework taut inside the display frame and should be made of wood.

To determine the size stretcher you will need, measure your finished needlework size by pulling the work to shape vertically and horizontally to see how it will best be presented, remembering that the lip of the display frame will cover about 1/8 inch (3.175 mm) all around (Fig. 2-4a). For needlepoint you will make the stretcher frame to fit the worked part of the canvas. Manufacturers of needlework kits often suggest frame size on the instruction sheet, and some crewelwork and cross-stitch fabrics have markings for corners or centers. Always measure the work with a slight stretch to see that the manufacturer is correct and that the

FIGURE 2-4.
MAKING A STRETCHER FRAME FOR NEEDLE WORK.

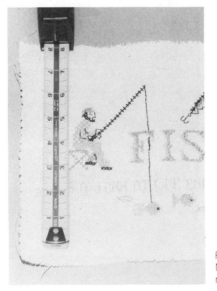

FIGURE 2-4a.
Measure the size you wish the needlework to be, length and width.

markings will not show. It is well to remember that ready-made frames are available only in standard sizes, and even if you do not plan to use a ready-made, these standard sizes have proven to be pleasingly proportioned, so check out the possibility of stretching the work to one of these sizes (see page 28).

For the stretcher frame, you may purchase artists' stretcher strips, available in art supply stores, or lattice wood, sold in long lengths in lumberyards. Artists' stretcher strips are used for stretching paintings on canvas and come in sizes by the inch. You will need two for the sides and two for the top and bottom. They have the advantage of being strong and ready for use without being cut but the disadvantages of being thick (limiting the later choice of frame for the work) and of being available only by the inch (so that they are not versatile to subtlety in size).

To use stretcher strips, slip the side and top together, forming an L, repeat this procedure for the other side and bottom (see Fig. 2-2a), then join the two L's together to form a rectangle. Using a T square, make sure that the four corners are at right angles and are tightly together.

A fine alternative to stretcher strips is lattice wood. The best kind is 5/16 inch by 1-5/8 inch (7.94 mm × 4.11 cm), but this is not as readily available as the standard 1/4 inch by 1-1/2 inch (6.35 mm × 3.81 cm). You might try a specialty lumber company, one that sells house-trimming woods, for the heavier lattice. The narrow one will do, however, except for large needleworks or needlepoint, which is out of shape when being stretched. To use lattice wood, determine your length and width measurements as before. If you have a miter box, cut the pieces so that the outsides of the mitered corners are equivalent to your finished-piece measurements (Fig. 2-4b), then join them together with Elmer's glue and

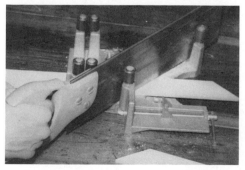

FIGURE 2-4b.
Cut pieces of lattice wood so that outer corners match measurements for the needleword stretcher frame.

75

staple each corner on the front and back (Fig. 2-4c). If you do not have a miter box, cut the pieces squarely with a saw, making each piece one lattice-wood width smaller than the measurements you need, then join with Elmer's glue and staples at perfect right angles to form your stretcher frame (Fig. 2-4d).

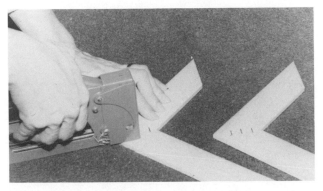

FIGURE 2-4c.
Glue, then staple corners of lattice frame on both sides.

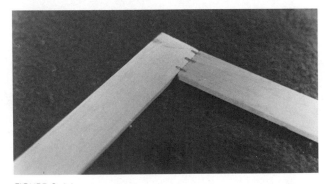

FIGURE 2-4d.
If you do not have a miter box, cut the corners bluntly, then join as shown.

When you have constructed your stretcher frame, you will need a white backing of poster board, scrap mat board, or mounting board, no more than 1/8 inch (3.175 mm) thick, cut to the size of the stretcher frame to act as a backing for your work. If you are anxious to preserve your needlework for many years, you should use 100 percent rag acid-free board, as described on page 12, or you may use in its place a white cotton that has been washed many times. Otherwise the impurities that are present in cardboards may be isolated from your stitchery by spraying with a clear plastic spray, also available in art supply and hobby stores, but this is only a temporary protective measure. If you have a fairly large needlework or one which will need an extra-strong stretcher frame, glue the backing to the frame with Elmer's glue and weigh down until dry. (Fig. 2-4e.)

FIGURE 2-4e.
Cut a white backing to fit the stretcher frame.

Any needlework you are stretching will need a border at least 1 inch (2.54 cm) larger than your stretcher frame in order to allow for pulling. If your border is not that wide, you will have to sew an extra piece of strong-bodied fabric to the outer edges (Fig. 2-5). When you are ready to stretch your fabric, center it first on the frame, carefully measuring by eye or ruler if necessary so that you have a

FIGURE 2-5.
If the needlework needs larger borders for pulling, sew an extra piece of mat material to each side, then topstitch as shown.

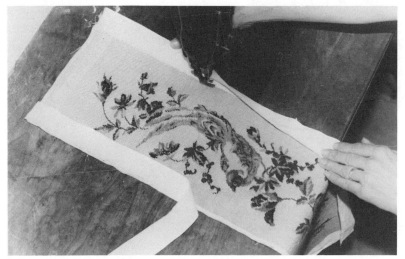

77

basic idea of where it should be placed on the frame. Allow for stretchability by pulling to a reasonable tightness in both up-and-down and crosswise directions. When you are reasonably sure about placement, staple one corner down on both sides (Fig. 2-6a). Following the grain as closely as possible, pull slightly, line up, and staple the next corner (in a clockwise movement). Then follow with the opposite two corners, watching the pattern and threads as much as you can at this stage. (Stapling on the sides of your stretcher frame will allow you a much more accurate lining up of the grain than stapling in back, and if you are framing the work, the staples will be covered.) If the piece looks well centered after this, you then proceed with one side and staple from one corner to the next with staples at regular intervals (Fig. 2-6b), the finer the fabric the closer together, until you reach the corner. Check to see that you've placed the second-corner staples correctly before proceeding around the piece. The final side is usually the tightest, but unless you are working with a very heavy piece, such as needlepoint, you shouldn't need to have the work overly tight.

FIGURE 2-6. STRETCHING NEEDLEWORK.

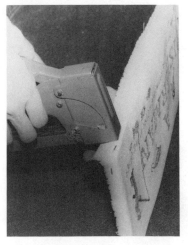

FIGURE 2-6a.
Center, stapling corners first.

When stretching needlepoint, simply stretch the fabric lining up the worked part of the canvas with the front edge of the stretcher frame. With needlepoint as with canvas, canvas pliers, which are sold in art supply stores, can be a godsend to help line up the stitches correctly.

After you have completed your stretching, check to see how well you have lined up the design. Here is where you can do some

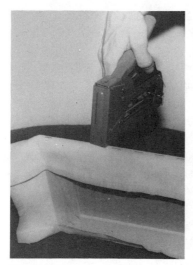

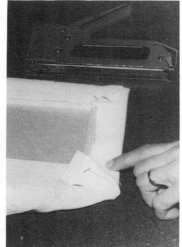

FIGURE 2-6b.
Pull slightly, line up, and staple sides.

FIGURE 2-6c.
Staple extra fabric to back.

adjusting. Unfortunately, some designs do not follow the grain of the fabric, and in these you must simply place the picture properly without regard to grain. The nicest-looking stretch jobs are done with the grain as much as possible, and usually the pictures fall into place.

The most difficult needleworks to stretch are those that have straight-line designs or borders, and those that are out of shape. Many needlepoints will need to be blocked before stretching. With straight-line borders, such as those on many cross-stitch samplers, it is well not to stretch them too tightly and to follow their grain very closely with staples close together, then to readjust later until they are in line. Leaving them slightly less than perfect can be an enhancement, even though this may seem a flaw to you, for it is one of the paradoxes of aesthetics that slight irregularities make for charm and beauty. Perfect lines can make a piece appear machine-made and sometimes lifeless.

When you have finished stretching, turn the work over on a clean surface and staple the border fabric to the back of the stretcher frame (Fig. 2-6c).

BLOCKING NEEDLEPOINT
Many needlepoints are out of shape when they are completed because of uneven tensions in their stitches. They take on, in vary-

ing degrees, a diamond shape. These pieces cannot readily be stretched but must be brought into a perfect rectangular or square shape by a process known as blocking. To block is to square off the needlepoint by wetting or steaming it, then securing it in the proper shape to a board until dry. Not many needleworks need to blocked, only those that are solid fabricwork on needlepoint canvas, such as needlepoint or pullthread.

To block needlepoint, you must first determine that all yarns, markings, and canvases are colorfast. Often instructions in your kit will indicate this. Test each yarn separately in cold water and blot with a white towel. All your own markings, such as date and signature should have been done with a marker designed for needlework use and should be colorfast. In badly-out-of-shape needlepoint that is not colorfast you should steam the work and block without wetting.

As in stretching, your work must have a border of at least 1 inch (2.54 cm) for pulling. You will need a blocking board. A very fine adjustable board can be constructed from four pieces of lattice wood approximately 24 inches (61 cm) long, or a size a bit longer than the work you usually do, and a piece of plywood, also available in the lumberyard. Nail the lattice to the plywood with short nails in whatever position you will need for the present blocking. Place the lattice frame about 1 inch longer than the longest length and 1 inch wider than the widest width of your work at perfect right angles and nail down (Fig. 2-7a). Later you can pry them up and adjust them for other needlepoint blocking. The

FIGURE 2-7.
BLOCKING NEEDLEPOINT.

FIGURE 2-7a.
This reusable blocking board is our own invention and is made of plywood and lattice secured with short tacks.

conservationists won't disapprove of this kind of blocking board—it will allow for air circulation and will facilitate drying as well as square off your work. Stretcher strips will serve the same purpose but are more expensive if you are to block many pieces, because you will always have to have new ones.

Determine the shape the piece should be, either by the directions or by the design itself. Do not go to extremes in blocking a piece if it will be overstretched to reach the size you want. You must work with it to make it look its best. You will have to work with the longest sides, because you cannot shorten them in blocking, but will have to stretch the shorter sides to these longer lengths. If you wish, you can make a grid on the plywood board for measuring purposes.

Immerse the whole piece in cold water and let it soak until it is entirely saturated (Fig. 2-7b), then remove it to a clean towel with-

FIBURE 2-7b.
Dunk the needlepoint in water and let it soak until thoroughly saturated.

out wringing or overly squeezing and roll it up carefully for a few minutes. When you are ready to block, place the piece on the blocking board and carefully line up the edge adjoining the longest side at the widest angled corner, with the corners exactly where they should fall in the blocking device, 1/2 inch (1.27 cm) from the lattice. It may help to have waterproof centers marked on the board and the needlepoint canvas sides in order to line everything up. Staple this first edge across to the lattice at approximately 1/2-inch (1.27-cm) intervals. Next, staple the largest edge in the same manner. Be sure the needlework does not remain in contact with the wood, as this would flatten the stitches or cause stains in that area. Secure the three corners you have worked up to into perfect right angles (Fig. 2-7c). The final corner is the one opposite the longest side, and this can be quite a lot of work to get into place. After you have stapled all sides into place and the piece is squared off, add extra staples where it looks even slightly bowed in (Fig. 2-7d). The work will retain the exact shape you have blocked it into, so do it as carefully square and straight-lined as you can. Let it dry completely and then stretch on a stretcher frame as described.

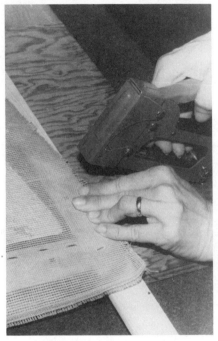

FIGURE 2-7c.
Staple one side, then square off all the corners into place.

FIGURE 2-7d.
When the piece is all lined up, staple all the places that bow in, then let dry in a horizontal position, and stretch as in Figure 2-6.

NEEDLEWORK: OTHER METHODS OF PREPARATION

Most needlework is stretched on a stretcher frame and then placed into the final frame in much the same manner as an oil painting, with no glass or mat. There are cases, however, that require special handling: when you feel the absolute necessity for the color note of a mat; when the needlework is so fragile that it cannot be stretched in this manner; or, in the case of silk, when stapling presents a snagging hazard. These three forms of needlework framing call for special techniques.

MATTING NEEDLEWORK

We hold the opinion that needlework SHOULD NOT be matted, at least not with a cardboard mat. The reasons for this should be apparent by now. Paper needs to be framed under glass, whereas cloth does not. Naturally when you use a mat on a needlework, you must decide between the two. If you decide in favor of the work and use no glass, your mat is vulnerable to humidity and other destructive influences and in time will pull away from the needlework and leave unsightly gaps. Because most mats are dyed in fashionable colors for decorative purposes with dyes that are "fugitive," that is, which fade when exposed to light and air, they will lose their crisp color in a relatively short time. Because they are made of wood-pulp paper, they can actually stain the cloth they touch. (And aside from the technical difficulty involved, as well as all the other arguments, it is in questionable taste to use paper borders around cloth works, in our opinion.) Since we like to recommend methods of framing that are relatively permanent, we would suggest that you use glass if you insist upon a mat.

Since the mat itself must be supported all around the picture image, we have found it best to stretch the needlework on a flat surface such as a canvas panel in a size large enough for the mat to rest on. Canvas panels are canvas-surfaced stiff cardboard panels that have been primed with gesso for artists' use. We feel they are appropriate because they are easily available, they are rigid, and especially because they are primed. This isolates the stitchery from impurities in the cardboard core. Never use corrugated board for stretching, because the glue that is used in its manufacture is highly acidic and will stain your work.

FIGURE 2-8.
MATTING NEEDLEWORK

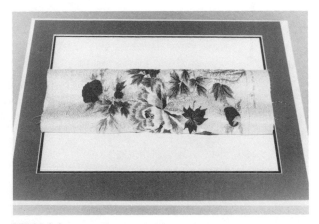

FIGURE 2-8a.
Cut the mat first, then use a canvas panel to stretch the
needlework.

First, determine the mat size and cut the mat. See our chapters on proportion and mat cutting. Select a canvas panel from your local art supply store in a size slightly smaller than your mat (Fig. 2-8a). You can use a larger panel and cut it down later with a utility knife, but it isn't easy. Center the needlework image over the panel using the mat to place it properly. Staple the piece from the front, starting with the corners, then pulling the sides into place, in much the same fashion as you would do stretcher stapling (Fig. 2-8b). It may help to mark your panel at the corners where the

FIGURE 2-8b.
Staple the needlework to the panel, using a ruler, if
necessary, to line up the area the mat will expose.

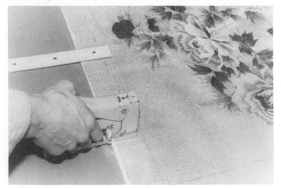

FIGURE 2-8c:
Stapled needlework.

FIGURE 2-8d.
Using double-faced tape, secure the mat in place around the work, then trim the bucking panel if it is too large.

image is to line up with the mat opening. After the needlework has been stretched tightly and in a perfect rectangle, cut off any excess fabric and backing (Fig. 2-8c). Line the entire inside opening of the mat with double-faced tape and press into place (Fig. 2-8d). Using glass, frame the matted piece in the same way you would a matted work on paper.

ANTIQUE OR FRAGILE PIECES

Some stitchery by its very nature cannot or should not be stretched. Openwork pieces such as tatting or crochet, antique or fragile samplers, and pieces that have lovely finished borders should be presented in their entirety and should be handled in a shadow box technique—a technique described in Chapter 3.

They are sewn to a fabric-mounted backing and set into a frame with glass removed preferably 1/2 inch (1.27 cm). (See Fig. 3-4.) The experts recommend air holes in the back of the frame for air circulation.

SILK

Silk embroidery and painting should be stretched in a unique manner, without the use of staples. You may or may not choose to mat this work, but we generally frame it under glass in either case, with some method of removal from the glass (Remember, no artwork of any medium should rest directly against glass.)

To stretch silk, you will need a rigid backing, such as a mounting board, with a white surface. Preferably you should face this backing with a sheet of museum board in order to isolate and protect the silk from the cardboard. Cut the board approximately 1 inch (2.54 cm) smaller all around than the silk piece, using judgment about the size you want it to be if you plan to leave the piece unmatted. If the silk has creases or wrinkles, steam it first (Fig. 2-9a). Make a line of Elmer's glue on one back edge of your mounting board (Fig. 2-9b). Line up the silk piece on the front, folding the edge of the silk over the prepared edge of the mounting board, and smooth into place (Fig. 2-9c). When this edge is firmly dry and secure, turn to the opposite side and repeat this procedure, pulling the silk to a gentle tautness, with allowance for vertical and horizontal stretching. Do this with the two remaining edges, then glue the corners into place (Fig. 2-9d).

FIGURE 2-9. SILK.

FIGURE 2-9a.
If the silk has creases, it may help to steam it first.

FIGURE 2-9b.
Cut a mounting board to approximately 1 inch (2.54 cm) smaller all around than the silk. Turn over and make a line of Elmer's on one back edge.

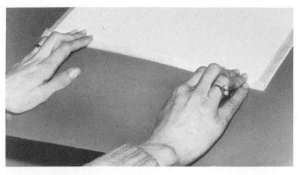

FIGURE 2-9c.
Place the silk face up on the right side of the board, turn
the silk's edge over the mounting board and glue down.

FIGURE 2-9d.
Pulling slightly, repeat this with the opposite end, then the other
two sides. Finished stretching will resemble this.

SPECIAL EFFECTS

When a frame alone does not seem enough or when
the piece seems too enclosed and needs added width, unusual
effects can be achieved in the framing of needlework by using
cloth-clad liners, panels in double frames, or by stretching the
fabric over a layer of foam.

LINERS

Wonderful, even spectacular, results can be achieved in the framing of needlecraft, with the use of a liner inside the outer frame.
This is technically 100 percent better than matting for perma-

nence and is really the proper way to add an enhancing color note and transition from work to frame molding. You may use a narrow, spray-painted band of color as a liner or a wider cloth-covered one (see Fig. 2-1). The 1/2-inch (1.27-cm) size corner-guard builders' molding can serve as the smaller liner, primed, then enamel-spray-painted. For a cloth-covered liner, follow the principles demonstrated in Figure 2-10 using linen, velvet, or any fabric complementary in texture and color to your work. We have found that natural-fiber cloths are more suitable than synthetics be-

FIGURE 2-10. MAKING A LINER.

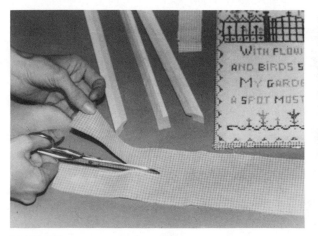

FIGURE 2-10a.
Cut strips of cloth wide enough to cover the face of the liner and wrap them around and under the lip.

FIGURE 2-10b.
Spread Elmer's glue over the face of the liner.

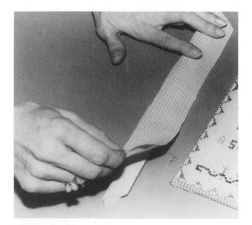

FIGURE 2-10c.
Smooth the cloth into place, watching the grain closely.

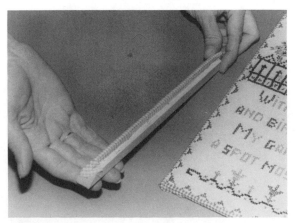

FIGURE 2-10d.
Glue and fold the cloth under the lip of the liner and then the corners.

FIGURE 2-10e.
Join the liner into a frame, then build the outer frame to fit it.

cause they have a more irregular weave and are more success-
fully glued down.

To cover a liner, cut four strips of cloth on the grain approximately
1/2-inch (1.27-cm) wider and longer than the liner molding (Fig.
2-10a). Spread a thin, uniform layer of Elmer's glue over the entire
face of the molding (Fig. 2-10b). Be sure the glue is even, with no
puddles nor dry spots. Working quickly, center the fabric over the
glue, leaving enough fabric on the lip side to go underneath but
not enough to touch the inner rabbet edge (Fig. 2-10c). Press the
fabric into place, smooth down, and let dry. Turn the molding over
and make a bead of glue all along the bottom of the lip, spread
smoothly, then fold the cloth over and, pulling gently, press into
place. When this is dry, glue each end of fabric as shown (Fig.
2-10d) by folding over. Join the liner frame (Fig. 2-10e).

If this is neatly done, it can be very professional looking—just the
right addition to a fine frame job. A liner can be used with an oil or
acrylic painting or on a needlework, but good taste tells us that it
should not be used in combination with a mat on paperwork.

DOUBLE FRAMES

Another good method of bringing out color in your needlework is
to use a double frame with a colored flat panel or a single frame
with a colored center panel (see Fig. 1-18). The double frame is in a
flat, wide form, emphasizing flatness of design, which would usually

prove more complementary to contemporary or nonperspective designs (Fig. 2-11). It is made up of an inner molding to hold the picture, a flat panel, and an outer complementary molding around the panel.

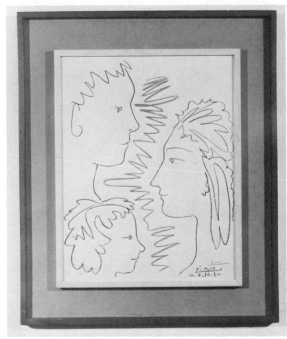

FIGURE 2-11.
Pablo Picasso: "La Mere et les Enfants."
Lithograph (1961).
Collection of the authors.

FOAM BACKING

For a time many professionals were stretching all their needlework over a 1/4-inch (6.35-mm) layer of mounting foam. This material gives a soft, smooth effect, absorbing knots in back of the work, raising the stitches slightly in a pleasing manner, and showing a beveled edge all around the edge of the work next to the frame.

Although it is a lovely way of presenting cloth-based work such as cross-stitch and crewel, its stability as a backing is questionable, as well as its long-term effect on the needlework itself. We've all seen foam rubber that has been exposed to air take on a chrome-yellow color in a relatively short time and subsequently disintegrate. It also tends to gather and to hold moisture. For these reasons we do not recommend its use. If you do have a decorative, fun piece on a background other than white and wish to use foam, here's how: Make your stretcher frame as usual and glue a cardboard panel of the same size to its front. Cut a piece of foam no thicker than 1/4 inch (6.35 mm) a little larger than the stretcher frame. Use a spray glue all over the cardboard face and press the foam into place. Trim the edges and stretch your needlework, a little less tight than usual, over the foam-covered stretcher frame.

▌SELECTING THE COMPLEMENTARY FRAME

We have discussed in detail the principles of choosing frames for both paper and canvas works, and these same basic principles apply to needlework. Generally speaking, there ARE some points peculiar to this craft to consider. Since glass is not normally used and since needlework has no shiny varnish as do some paintings, the work usually has a matte appearance, which makes shiny-finished moldings appear somewhat out of place. Since it is not matted, it looks best in a frame larger than that of the equivalent-size drawing, but smaller than the equivalent-size painting. Since it is usually somewhat naïve in character, a very "sophisticated"-looking frame may not be in keeping. Simple design flat- and scoop-shape frames at least 1 inch wide, depending of course on the piece, with matte finishes are often the best choices (Fig. 2-12). A colored panel in the wood is quite often just the right finishing touch.

FIGURE 2-12.
Blackwork Sampler. Black thread on linen (1978).
Lent by Mrs. F. S. Frankland.

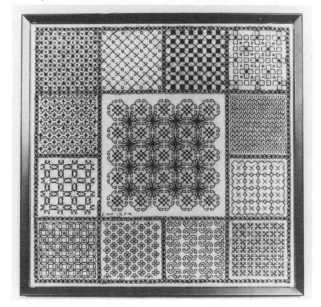

FITTING THE NEEDLEWORK INTO THE FRAME

Many frames are deep-rabbeted, allowing the needlework with its stretching device to be set into the frame with room to spare, and if this is so, you will simply tack the piece in with brads as you would any other kind of work and cover the back with paper (see Fig. 1-21). But in most instances the stretcher and the bulk of the work will fill the entire rabbet and then some. Here you will set the piece into the frame and then staple the wooden stretcher strips to the frame's back (Fig. 2-13).

FIGURE 2-13.
If the needlework fills the frame's rabbet completely, staple it in.

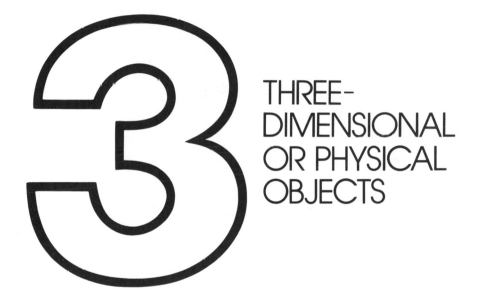

3 THREE-
DIMENSIONAL
OR PHYSICAL
OBJECTS

The framing of three-dimensional or physical objects, such as artifacts, plates, or coins, is accomplished by securing the objects to a stiff backing, which is usually covered with some appropriate cloth or enhancing material, then set into a frame with or without the use of glass.

FIGURE 3-1.
American Indian artifacts (fragments of pottery and spearheads). Courtesy of Schmidt Hose.

SHADOW BOXES

When you wish to display a three-dimensional object in a frame, you would place it into a boxlike frame known as a shadow box. A shadow box is a frame with a rabbet deep enough to contain the object itself and the backing on which it is mounted, and to allow space between the glass and the object (when glass is used). Pieces such as plates, guns, coins, medals, and fans are framed in shadow boxes, but the technique can be used in lieu of matting for glass removal from prints, photos, or cloth pieces also. It is a simple but invaluable technique to know for fine framing. There is great leeway for creative expression in shadow box framing, for there are unlimited possibilities for design, placement, and materials.

The typical shadow-boxing materials you will need are: a frame with adequate rabbet; a mounting board such as plywood, Upson board, or Fome-Cor board (depending on the weight of the object); balsa wood for glass removal; glass; and a fabric to line the inner surfaces for added beauty of display (Fig 3-2a).

Three-Dimensional
or Physical Objects

FIGURE 3-2.
SHADOW BOX.

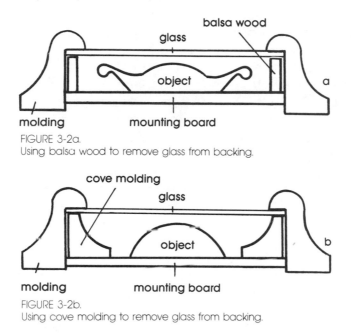

FIGURE 3-2a.
Using balsa wood to remove glass from backing.

FIGURE 3-2b.
Using cove molding to remove glass from backing.

Although the inner surfaces can be painted or covered with a colored mat board, cloth is usually the richest looking. A more complex shadow box can be achieved with the use of a cove or scoop molding for glass removal (Fig. 3-2b).

In choosing the frame for your shadow box, you will have to do some precise measuring to be sure that the molding has an adequate but not exaggerated rabbet depth. The object should not touch the glass, but not be set so far back that it appears to be in a tunnel. Usually 1/4 inch (6.35 mm) to 1/2 inch (1.27 cm) is an adequate distance between highest object surface and glass. The mounting board should not exceed a thickness of 3/8 inch (1 cm) for ease of handling and weight. For lightweight objects 1/4-inch (6.35-mm) Fome-Cor board is to be recommended. Not only is it featherweight, rigid, and easily cut or hollowed out, but it can be sewn through. We use it for mounting coins, medals, stitchwork, fans, and anything else that is lightweight. Sometimes we use strips of it to line the sides of the shadow box frame to hold the glass, instead of balsa wood.

Plates, guns, and other heavy pieces require a wooden mounting board for support, and 3/8-inch (1-cm) plywood is our suggestion. If you do use plywood, you will need a good saw and, in the case of plates, a saber saw to cut the circular opening. Sometimes you can substitute several layers of mounting board glued together if they seem heavy enough. Once you have selected the appropriate backing, measure its thickness, the height or thickness of the object to be framed, add 1/8 inch (3.175 mm) for glass and 1/4 inch (6.35 mm) to 1/2 inch (1.27 cm) for space, and these totaled with room in back to set the piece into the frame will determine the molding's rabbet depth (see Figs. 1-16 and 3-2).

In shadow boxes you must be certain to place the objects well, not only in good arrangement, proportion, and centering where necessary but also in perfect horizontal or vertical positions or, in the case of round objects such as coins or plates, in a perfectly upright position with top and center bottom in a straight line with these centers of the mounting board. It is very frustrating to discover that the object is incorrectly placed once the entire job is done. Another word of advice in the framing of artifacts is that they should be tastefully and simply presented as what they are and not in faddish positions. Work with the object you are mounting, using the most logical way. If the object has open places or is cloth, thus making it suitable for sewing, use transparent thread or fishing line, depending on the weight, to secure it to the backing. If it has only a solid surface, like a plate or a stone, use L-shaped nails to support it and perhaps a dab of silicone glue. If parts of it seem to need to be mounted below the surface of the mounting board, make indentations or hollow out the backing for these parts to rest in. If it has a natural hanging device of its own, make use of this in mounting. The saber in Figure 3-3 has two loops on

FIGURE 3-3.
Saber. Lent by Richard Britnell.

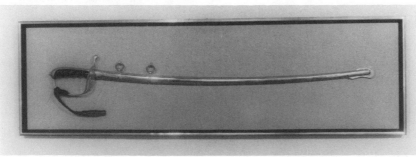

Three-Dimensional
or Physical Objects

top designed to fit hooks on the belt for carrying. We used two screw hooks in the mounting board to hold these loops, then added a padded bent nail at the pointed end to balance the sword in the frame. This piece was framed without glass, making it easy to remove for polishing. Make note of all the framing requirements for your particular project—glass versus no glass, weight, shape, nice presentation, and so on—then use your own common sense in mounting it. In framing physical objects as well as in other framing, being in tune with the nature of the piece and using common sense bring the best results, as naturally this is the basis for all good construction. Above all, devise a plan that will cause no permanent harm to the object. Present objects simply and unpretentiously, without exaggeration of proportion, taking care to make the backing a comfortable width, neither so confining nor so wide as to be disturbing. Unless the work itself is humorous or decorative in nature, do not place it (or them) in a faddish position in the name of being "artistic." If you decide to off-center, tilt, or stagger placements, work a long time to be sure the work is in balance; otherwise you will be forever wanting to lift one side of the picture.

If you are not using glass, choose a molding that has a back high enough to raise the face of the molding to the same level as or higher than the object's top surface (see Fig. 1-16), so that the object is set back and contained —nestled, if you will—and not jutting out from the frame.

SUITABLE DISPLAY FABRICS
AND HOW TO MOUNT THEM

The fabric you choose to line your shadow box will depend largely upon the nature of the piece you are framing. Velvet and satin, of course, are very formal, while felt and burlap are not. Cotton, linen, and unusual fabrics such as suede make fine display fabrics. Texture and color available will be your main concerns, and you may have to make compromises to achieve the look you want. For example, the fabric used in a fan we framed was a synthetic, chosen for the color. We used the wrong side of the fabric for the display side, because the right side was too shiny and regular looking in the weave to be attractive for framing purposes. Generally, natural fabrics are better for framing than synthetics, and in choosing the one best for your particular job, try to choose a texture that best expresses the nature of the piece. For example, for the Indian artifacts (see Fig. 3-1) we used burlap, whereas in presenting the plate in Figure 3-5 we chose felt. Furthermore, color should accentuate and offset the object but should be in keeping with the room in which the piece is to be displayed.

First you must determine the arrangement of the object or objects to be framed, then measure for the supporting backing (mounting board). This shape will naturally determine the finished frame size, so the proportion should follow the dictates of good design. Cut the backing, then cut the fabric to a size larger than the backing. With Elmer's glue and a paintbrush or small paint roller, coat the front of the mounting board evenly without leaving any puddles or dry spots. It is exactly the same procedure as followed in the covering of a mat. Use only enough glue to accomplish the job and no more, or you will end up with stains in the fabric. Apply the fabric and pat into place, avoiding any bubbles (see Fig. 1-11). Weigh it down under a flat surface, such as glass, until dry. It is important to work quickly and have everything in readiness, for the glue dries quickly. Take care that the glue is distributed completely to the edges of the board and is very evenly applied. For a professional appearance, place the cloth carefully, lining up its grain with the mounting board.

For a very refined piece of work, you may choose to use silk or another delicate fabric. In this case, you will mount the fabric in the manner illustrated in Figure 2-9.

HOW TO MOUNT OBJECTS
Good framing practices require that we present the object to its very best advantage with a minimum of harm done to it. In the case of valuable work, no permanent damage of any kind should occur in framing. Most shadow-boxing can be done without damaging the object or altering its original condition in any way. The pieces we describe are those most commonly framed, and this is our normal mounting procedure.

ARTIFACTS. Rigid three-dimensional artifacts, which are solid material such as stone, clay, or glass, often cannot be sewn or tied to the mounting board, but must be anchored there by some means other than glue or hollowing out of the board. Museums use this simple procedure: Cut the tops off of brads that are strong enough to support the weight of the object in question and bend them at right angles in an L shape. Using a plywood board as the backing, determine placement of the object in the board and mark where the brads should be placed to hold it there. Remove the object and hammer the brads into the board. Then put the object in place and turn the L-shaped brads to hold it there. If this seems insufficient, you may use a dot of silicone glue to help hold the object more securely. When the securing is done, paint the brads a color that blends with the object to make them invisible.

ANTIQUE OR FRAGILE CLOTH PIECES. Fragile or antique stitchery and oddly shaped cloth pieces can be sewn to the mounting board if you use Fome-Cor board as your backing. To place the stitches properly, it may be advantageous to place guideholes through the backing with a T pin (Fig. 3-4a) before sewing. Once your

FIGURE 3-4.
ANTIQUE OR FRAGILE CLOTH PIECES.

FIGURE 3-4a.
Use a T pin to penetrate the mounting board to facilitate sewing.

display fabric has been mounted to the board, place the stitchery properly and carefully sew it onto the backing with a transparent thread, stitching only the parts that need support around the edges and a few in the center if they seem necessary to avoid uneven tensions in the future (Fig. 3-4b). Only pull the threads tight enough to hold the piece, not to show tension. A fabric backing with clinging or frictional qualities of its own, such as velvet or felt, can be an aid in keeping the piece in place as well.

PLATES. Collector plates or bowls with artful designs make beautiful

FIGURE 3-4b.
Sew the piece to the mounting board with transparent thread.

and unusual wall adornments when used sparingly and in good taste. For many contemporary dishes, standard-size round frames are available that you can simply clamp your plate into and hang. But the unparalleled drama and setting provided by a cloth-lined shadow box in a square or rectangular shape can be so breathtakingly exquisite that you should make a special effort to see one presented in this manner before resorting to the round frame. The process of shadow-boxing a plate is rather complex, but the results are worth it.

The most commonly used mounting backboard for pottery is 3/8-inch (1-cm) plywood, or a thickness equal to the depth of the plate's base, but to use it, you need access to a good saw to cut the basic right-angle shape and a saber saw to cut a round opening in the board for the base of the plate to fit into. If you do not have these cutting tools, you may substitute two thicknesses of 3/16-inch (4.763-mm) Upson board, available in lumberyards, or three thicknesses of mounting board, sold in art supply stores, which can be cut separately with a utility knife and then glued together to make a sturdy backing. These cardboard substitutes should be used only for lighter-weight dishes. If the plate has identifying information or the potter's signature on the bottom, this can be made visible from the back, as a charming touch, by cutting a "porthole" opening the size of the pot's base in the back cover with a Plexiglas cover to insulate. A ceramic does not need glass for protection but is usually framed under glass anyway when shadow-boxed in order to protect the lining fabric from dust and moisture, and it may extend the life of the plate itself it there are atmospheric impurities in the area in which it is to hang.

Measure for your backboard allowing enough room all around the plate for an offsetting border. Since plates require a deeply rabbeted frame; ample breathing room will keep it from looking closed in. A square shape is logical, but you may prefer to elongate the sides or top and bottom for a specific display area.

Once your backboard shape is cut, measure the plate's base (from flare to flare) and add 1/8 inch (3.175 mm) for allowance. This measurement will be the diameter of the round opening you will cut in the backboard for the plate's base to rest in. Place your straightedge diagonally across the board from one corner to opposite corner and draw a line, then repeat with the other two corners. The intersection point of these two lines marks the center of the board, and this is the center point of the circle you will cut for the plate's base. Using a compass, open to a width of half the measurement you have determined for the plate's base (plus 1/8-inch [3.175-mm] allowance), insert the compass point into the center point on the board, and draw the circle. Measure it to be sure the diameter is correct. If you are using plywood, drill a hole in the board inside on the circled line to make a place for the saber saw blade to enter, then cut the circle out with the saw. If you are using cardboard, cut the circle out with a utility knife.

Mount the lining fabric over the board as described in the previous section and allow to dry. Trim the fabric around the outer edges of the mounting board, then cut the center out and trim completely to the circle's edge (Fig. 3-5).

You are now ready to mount the plate into the backboard. The museums mount their creamics without glues and only by means of holders such as the nails we described on page 99, using two supporting L-shaped-nails on the bottom and one on the top. If you wish, you may use this method, but remember that museum pieces are not moved around too often and are kept in stationary cases. For framing, a silicone glue is practical to hold the plate in place. It is a liquid rubber that dries to a transparent hardness, clinging firmly to the ceramic but remaining flexible and removable if the need arises. With the board face up on your worktable, place the plate into the circular opening. Carefully adjust the

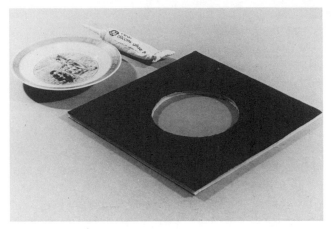

FIGURE 3-5.
Mounting a plate. After cutting a circular opening in the mounting
board and covering the board with fabric, insert the plate's
base and secure with L-shaped nails or silicone glue.

plate, centering top and bottom to align with center top and
bottom of the board, because in the finished frame job the face
of the plate will appear exactly as you place it in the frame. It may
be helpful to make small center markings on the edges of the
board and on the plate with a wax crayon.

When you are sure the placement is correct, cover the plate with
a sheet of glass approximately the size of the mounting board;
then, holding the glass and backboard with the plate
sandwiched between them, reverse the entire unit so that the
bottom of the backboard is on top and the glass is on the bottom.
Squeeze a line of silicone glue all around the base of the plate,
binding it to the cut opening of the board. Carefully reverse the
unit once to be sure the centers are still in line, then replace it face
down and let it dry for twenty-four hours, or until the glue has set.
Then you are ready to frame the mounted plate.

COINS. Coins are easily mounted using Fome-Cor board, cloth, an
X-acto knife, and a pencil.

First plan the arrangement and cut the outer shape of Fome-Cor
board. Place the coins in the desired position and carefully delineate the position each one is to occupy on the board, using a
sharp pencil (Fig. 3-6a). Handle the coins with tissue paper to
avoid fingerprints. Remove the coins, and score the penciled-in

Three-Dimensional
or Physical Objects

circles with an X-acto knife, penetrating only the first paper layer of the Fome-Cor. Carefully deepen this cut and lift out the inner foam, making a hollowed-out round indenture for the coin to fit into (Fig. 3-6b). The object is to cut the top layer of paper and inside foam leaving the bottom layer intact. The coin should fit in easily, but not loosely, and the covering fabric will take up the slack and hold it firmly in place.

FIGURE 3-6.
MOUNTING COINS USING FOME-COR BOARD.

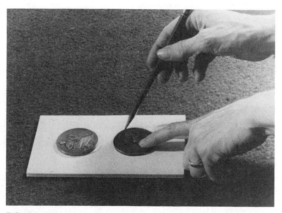

FIGURE 3-6a.
Delineate the placement of each coin with a sharp pencil.

FIGURE 3-6b.
Score the line with an X-acto knife and carefully lift out the center foam, leaving the bottom paper intact.

FIGURE 3-6c.
Cover the board with fabric, cut
an X into each opening and a slit
in each V, press into opening,
and insert coins.

When all the openings are hollowed out, mount the fabric as described earlier. Cut an X in the fabric center of each hollow place, then make a clip into the center of each V formed, and push the edges of the cloth down into the hollow. Insert the coin (Fig. 3-6c). The coin should pull the fabric to smoothness in the indenture and be firmly secure there, without the use of any adhesive (Fig. 3-7).

HOW TO ASSEMBLE A SHADOW BOX

The shadow box frame you have chosen must have, as stated, a rabbet adequate to house the object, glass, backing, and some leeway (1/4 inch [6.35 mm] to 1/2 inch [1.27 cm]) for separating and setting in.

Cut and join the frame to fit the backboard and cut the glass to fit well. Always use clear single-strength glass or Plexiglas in a shadow box, since you would not be able to see the objects through nonglare glass. In choosing the frame, you have allowed for the glass to be removed from the object, and now you must choose the proper removal device to fit the space between the backing and the glass and to hold them in place with the object between. Now measure the height (in relief) of the object, that is, how high its tallest point stands on top of the backing, and add the allowance between it and the glass, say 1/4 inch (6.35 mm). These two mea-

FIGURE 3-7.
Medals of commendation. Lent by Vivian Barr.

surements together determine the height of the balsa wood or
cove molding you will use for removal of backing from glass. Next
measure the lip of the molding's rabbet. A bit smaller than this, to
allow for fabric covering, will determine its width or thickness, so
that it is no wider than the lip.

Now cut four pieces of balsa wood to fit perfectly inside the rabbet of the frame. Cut them with blunt edges. (If you are using cove
molding, you will have to miter the corners, cover it with fabric, join,
and build the outer frame to fit the cove frame.) Cut four strips of
fabric wide enough to cover the balsa wood's face and fold over
the top, bottom, and two ends. This folding over of the fabric will
hide raw edges and present a neat, upholstered appearance.
Clean the glass now.

Spread Elmer's glue over the surface of the balsa wood, just as
you would when mounting the backing fabric, smoothly without
puddles, then put the fabric into place. When this is dry, put a thin

glue line on the top and bottom edges, smooth with the finger, and fold all the edges over. Trim the fabric to the wood lengthwise and trim to 1/4 inch (6.35 mm) of each end. Squeeze a line of glue on the raw wood side and spread over the surface smoothly; put each balsa wood piece into its place in the frame individually and hold there until the glue is set. Fold the loose cloth ends into place as each new piece is put in.

When all the inserts are in place and the glue has set, give the glass another light cleaning and dust the entire inner frame with a paintbrush. Clean the surface of the mounted object and backing thoroughly to clear it of particles. If the backing is velvet or has a tenuous quality, use a piece of Scotch tape to dab the particles off. Insert the mounted work into the frame and, if on examination all is right and clean, fasten it in with brads using a pair of pliers to avoid jarring (see Fig. 1-21). Finish the back with a paper cover or with a cloth-covered mounting board.

Three-Dimensional
or Physical Objects

4
MIRRORS OR PANELS

Mirrors, wooden and Masonite panels, stained-glass units, and other rigid self-supporting and self-sustaining flat objects are put directly into frames without backings or glass.

FIGURE 4-1.
Howard Ahrens: "David." Oil painting on panel (1939).
Lent by Miriam Ahrens.

MIRRORS

Because a mirror is heavier than most objects framed, especially if it is large, you must take extra care to choose a frame strong enough and to add reinforcements to help support its weight. Depending upon the size and weight, look for a hardwood molding, such as oak, maple, or walnut. Hardwood corners, when sanded smoothly, adhere better with glue than do softwoods. Glue should be used liberally in each mitered corner, and each corner should be permitted to dry thoroughly when making a frame for a mirror. Nails should be driven in vertically and horizontally on all the corners, and metal corner braces, available in any hardware store, should be used. The molding should be substantial in body for a very heavy mirror, and, even better than corner braces, you can cut a Masonite board measuring about 1/8 inch

(3.175 mm) smaller all around than the outer dimensions of the frame and glue, then screw it to the back of the finished product. You must use hanging devices especially designed for this purpose to hang a heavy mirror.

Mirrors have no permanent image and perhaps for this reason can sustain very ornate, even ostentatious frames if you wish. Many heavily carved or otherwise ornament-encrusted frames that we would now consider unsuitable for artwork make fine frames for mirrors.

PANELS

We have now come full circle back to the panel painting, which was really the first form of portable framed painting. Setting it into a frame probably has not changed much in six hundred years. Simply tack it in and add a paper dust cover if desired.

5

APPROACHING
THE PROFESSIONAL
PICTURE FRAMER

In recent years frame shops have proliferated and now are everywhere. Practically every town has a frame shop or two, either as part of another business or as an entity in itself. With this great number of framers and no regulations or standards to be met, there are bound to be some people who simply have set up shop without much knowledge of proper framing. All framers are not alike. So if you do decide to use the services of a professional, it is in your own best interest to do some investigating first. There are many reasons for going to a professional, among them the variety of combinations available, the finer finishes and styles of molding, and his or her general expertise in the field. Whatever your reason for going, you have the right to expect correct handling of your work, pleasing design, and a well-executed craft.

So, how do you find a good one? The best picture frame shops are usually acknowledged by local word of mouth. If you have a particularly valuable piece, you should consult your local museum or fine art gallery to find someone who specializes in conservation framing. Otherwise ask your neighbors and friends or colleagues, preferably people who have had a good many pictures framed, for their recommendations; most people who have had much work done will talk very enthusiastically about their favorite shops. But don't rely completely on their advice. It is a funny thing that very few people have discerning eyes in the area of picture framing. Almost any job is acceptable and praiseworthy unless it is glaringly remiss. The very same persons who have fine taste and demand quality and workmanship in home furnishings and dress are surprisingly unaware of quality differences in framing. So check out the prospective shop yourself, looking at the pictures in the gallery if there is one or the framed examples around the shop if there is not. Observe overall appearance of the frame jobs first. Are the selections (mat, frame, and so forth) tasteful and well combined in pleasing proportions and colors? Are the styles appropriate to their subject and in keeping with your own idea of what good framing should be? Next, take a closer look. Is the detail work—frame cornerwork, mat cutting—precisely executed? Is the frame molding itself of good quality? You can make pretty good judgments by outward appearance, not necessarily of the decor of the shop itself (for many a busy shop is not very tidy), but of the framed examples in it, much as you would select fresh vegetables in a produce market by their appearance. Meticulous, well-done work on the outside is a good sign that the inside

Approaching the Professional Picture Framer

is well done, too. If the shop passes this visual test, then question the framers or proprietors about their practices, asking them for their recommendations about handling your work, not only the choices of mat or frame but the materials and methods they will use in constructing your project. The more knowledgeable you are in this, the better equipped you are to recognize a good framer. A strong underlying intention of this book has been to inform you of good framing practices.

You are probably rather apprehensive if you are entering a frame shop for the first time, since you don't know what to expect and will be working with a stranger who will assist you and advise you about your framing. You may have a general idea of what you want, or no idea at all, and it is important that the framers or salespeople be sensitive to your responses as they show you things, but also that they be knowledgeable in guiding you to tasteful and practical choices. They will have in mind the technical requirements of your particular undertaking and keep you away from impractical decisions. If they have a very good eye and lots of experience, they will help you put together a beautiful object that suits you, your room, and your picture and that will offer you many years of pleasure.

If you have the sense that you are being pushed into a particular choice about which you have extreme reservations, you might well be wary. It is possible that the framer has an educated vision of how great the piece will look when done this way, but it is also possible that he has an oversupply of the particular material in question or stands to gain by its sale. Another shop to be suspicious of would be one where you are handled with indifference, which may well betoken the overall attitude of the shop. In fact it is best to visit several shops before settling on one.

Charges are another matter. Most of us have a budget that allows for a certain range of expenditure in each of our requirements, and, in the scheme of things, pictures and frames are usually considered a part of home furnishings. Most custom frame shops charge considerable sums for their work, charges that seem at first glance to be out of proportion to what is available in the general market of home items. Sometimes this criticism has validity; indeed, there are some shops that do "gouge" the public with prices inconsistent with the quality of work and materials used.

But we must come to the defense of the majority (we think) of framers, who try to make an honest living at this craft, with a word of explanation. First of all, there aren't many businesses left in which the work is done by hand and to specification. Custom fitting and putting together have been replaced by less expensive mass production in factories, where raw materials are purchased in volume and any handwork is done assembly-line-piecework style, each section of workers completing only one aspect of a uniform finished product. Although some large frame shops employ this method to an extent, the majority have one or two people doing each job to order from start to finish. This is by nature time-consuming: The more carefully done, the more time taken; and the more time taken, the more expensive to the business owner. You need only take a look at auto mechanics' or plumbers' bills to realize that their time and skill are more costly than their materials. Even the smallest shop has large overhead expenses—supplies, freight charges, rent, employees' salaries, taxes, insurance, licenses, utilities—which would astonish the layperson. And with the poor quality of many materials today, careful framers have to waste a great deal of the material they have paid for, cutting bad parts out of molding, and discarding soiled or damaged parts, even though they use short ends of molding, small pieces of glass, and scraps of mat board. After overhead and waste, with average pricing most framers make a profit of only a small percentage of their gross income, amounting to the equivalent of the average wage earner's salary, give or take a little. In fact, most professional picture framers are rather idealistic people who like to work with their hands creatively and be independent. Few of them get rich. In addition to all their other expenses, the materials they use can be costly. The better the quality, the more they must pay for them and the more they must charge for them. If they used fine-quality molding and excellent backing materials, they would be out of business very shortly if they could not receive a proportionally higher price for them than for moldings of less quality and ordinary corrugated-board backings. Most framers have to keep their prices competitive and are forced to use materials accordingly. They often have to compromise molding quality for price, and they use fine backing materials inside the frame only if they are requested or it is understood they will be used and added to the price. Many of the finest shops list the materials used on the back of the frame.

We are not recommending that you go out and find the most expensive frame shop in town, nor that you insist on the very finest materials available for every job you have done, because high price is not the criterion for locating a good framer and not every object is worthy of being framed with the finest materials. It is our firm conviction that if you can find an excellent craftsperson with a fine eye and a good knowledge of proper treatment, you will have a real value for your money.

GLOSSARY

ASSEMBLE: To put together the parts, such as the mat, picture, and backing.

AWL: A pointed tool for making holes in wood.

BACKING: Something forming a back for support. Usually this refers to the final stiff board used in framing papers.

BARRIER PAPER: A paper that has a neutral pH factor designed to separate the artwork from destructive materials.

BEVEL: An angled part or surface, usually referring to the angled cut of a mat opening.

BLOCK: In needlework framing, to wet and stretch the fabric into a square or rectangular shape.

BRAD: A thin nail with a small head.

BRAYER: A hard rubber roller with a handle, used to flatten paper or cloth.

CANVAS PLIERS: A tool with a wide grip for stretching canvas.

CLIP-IT: Trade name for a piece of hardware designed to fasten stretched canvas into the frame.

CONSERVATION: The official care and protection of natural resources.

CONSERVATION FRAMING: The framing of objects with materials and methods to preserve them.

DRY-MOUNT PRESS: A piece of equipment used to mount papers permanently by means of heat, adhesive, and pressure.

FITTING: Putting the prepared object into the frame.

FOME-COR: Trade name for a rigid, lightweight board made up of a polystyrene layer sandwiched between two smooth craft papers.

GESSO: A white base-coat paint used for priming canvas and for texturing woods.

GLASS CUTTER: A tool with a small sharp-edged metal wheel used to score glass before breaking.

HINGE: N. A small piece of paper or tape used to suspend paper or other material on a backing. V. To suspend a paper with the use of hinges.

JOIN: To put the mitered corners of a molding together permanently to form a frame.

LINER: A cloth-covered, painted, or finished wooden insert inside the frame opening used to separate the painting from the frame molding.

MAT: A colored cardboard into which a window is cut to make a border around a picture.

MAT BOARD: A cardboard with a colored or textured surface from which mats are made.

METAL LEAF: A very thin sheet of metal used to give the effect of gold or silver, usually to a frame.

MITER: A joint formed by fitting together two pieces (of molding) to form a corner.

MITER BOX: A piece of equipment with guides for a saw, used to cut the angles necessary for frame making.

MITER VISE: A device used to hold firmly in place two mitered molding pieces being joined.

MOLDING: A shaped strip of wood.

MOUNT: A general term meaning to secure an object to a backing or support.

MOUNTING BOARD: A board, often cardboard, used for mounting papers and other objects.

MUSEUM BOARD: A paper board made of cotton or other material that has a neutral pH factor and is designed for conservation framing and storing.

MUSEUM FRAMING: SEE Conservation framing.

NAIL SET: A metal tool with a blunt pointed end used to drive nails below the surface of the wood.

PANEL: A flat, rigid section, usually of wood or pressed wood and often in a rectangular shape. Also, the flat center of some frame moldings (panel frame).

PLEXIGLAS: A lightweight, transparent thermoplastic sheet.

PROFILE: An outline. In framing, an outline of molding shape.

RABBET: A cut made in the inside edge of a frame so that the picture may be fitted into it.

RAG PAPER: Paper made of cotton fibers.

REVERSE FRAME: A frame that slopes back to the wall with the picture projecting forward.

RICE PAPER: A machine-made or handmade Oriental paper. "Rice" paper is not made of rice, but usually of mulberry pulp.

SABER SAW: A hand-held power saw with a small blade capable of cutting curvilinear shapes.

SCOOP FRAME: A frame with its outer front edge away from the wall and its inner edge leading in to the picture.

SCREW EYE: A screw with a round loop end, designed for securing wire to the picture frame for hanging.

SHADOW BOX: A boxlike, deeply rabbeted frame used for the framing of three-dimensional objects.

STRETCHER FRAME: A wooden frame for stretching cloth, such as canvas, to smoothness.

UPSON BOARD: A particle board made up of wood chips pressed together.

UTILITY KNIFE: A sturdy knife with replaceable blades for cutting paper and other medium-weight materials.

WHEAT PASTE: A water-soluble paste made from wheat for gluing paper.

WOOD FINISH: The final outer appearance of a wooden surface, after staining, leafing, antiquing, and so on.

BIBLIOGRAPHY

ALBERS, JOSEF. Interaction of Color. New Haven: Yale University Press, 1971.

HEYDENRYK, HENRY. The Art and History of Frames. New York: James H. Heineman, Inc., 1963.

HEYDENRYK, HENRY. The Right Frame: A Consideration of the Right and Wrong Methods of Framing Pictures. New York: James H. Heineman, Inc., 1964.

HYDER, MAX. Picture Framing. New York: Pitman Publishing Corporation, 1963.

REINHARDT, ED, AND HAL ROGERS. How to Make Your Own Picture Frames. New York: Watson-Guptill Publications, 1958.

INDEX